NEW BUSINESS LANDMINES

The don'ts (and do's) for
starting & managing a small business

GARY R GROTTKE

Copyright © 2014 Gary R Grottke
All rights reserved.

ISBN 10: 150276542X
ISBN 13: 978-1502765420

Library of Congress Control Number: 2014918182
CreateSpace Independent Publishing Platform
North Charleston, South Carolina

To Karen
who supported me
as I threw away a six figure corporate job
to pursue my dream to
"be my own boss"
and
create something on my own.

Special thanks to
Candace Monteith, Hollie Bourne,
Sean Tegart, John Murphy and Bob Grottke
who took the time to read early versions of the book
and give me their thoughts and feedback.

Contents

Introduction		v
1	Everyone Says My Idea Is Great!	1
2	Who Needs a Business Plan?	10
3	A Bank Will Give Me the Money, Right?	27
4	Do I Need a Company?	33
5	Budgets Are Overrated!	45
6	What's SEO, a New Sports Drink?	49
7	Field of Dreams, or If I Build It, They Will Come	58
8	Set the Price High, so I Make Money!	70
9	I'll Do the Accounting in My Spare Time	80
10	Government Won't Bother Me—I'm a Little Guy!	84
11	Devil's Triangle: Lawyers, Lawsuits & Litigation	91
12	Just Buy a Business	103
13	He's My Friend, so We'll Be Good Partners	109
14	My Employees Will Love Me	127
15	What Does It All Mean?	135
About The Author		137
Exhibits		
A	Definitions of Business Jargon	139
B1/B2	Sample Business Plans	144
C	Sample Monthly Cash Flow Budget	180
D	Twelve-Week Cash Flow Forecast	185
E	List of Landmines	186

INTRODUCTION

A NEW RESTAURANT BLOWS all of its investment capital on just the space renovation, leaving no money for the start-up.

A new winery gets shut down because the owners didn't apply for a liquor license, and they were offering tastings.

A bowling alley floods. The result is a huge loss to the business because the new owner hadn't yet purchased property and casualty insurance.

Landmines! They blew up each of these new businesses.

These are true examples of business failures. Take note that none of these failures had anything to do with the core businesses—serving quality food and drinks, making wine, or offering recreation. There was nothing wrong with the product or service being offered. No, these businesses all failed because of stupid and avoidable mistakes.

> **Landmine #1:** *Many businesses fail not because of bad ideas, but because of poor execution.*

This book was written to help entrepreneurs avoid landmines due to poor execution.

Starting a new business is exhilarating, risky, and sometimes costly. It can also be very humbling at times. Most new businesses fail. In some industries, restaurants being an excellent example, failure rates exceed 50 percent. However, owning and managing a business can be financially and personally rewarding.

My personal experiences are broad based and somewhat unique. They have given me strong opinions about what to do and what not to do in business. Some of my entrepreneurial ventures have been successful; many others, complete failures. I hope to share these successes and failures and others that I have seen to help the reader be successful.

Someone who needs practical advice on how to start and launch his or her own business should be able to use this book as a self-help manual. The topics covered range from basic sales and marketing issues to legal and regulatory concerns. Advice will be offered on preparing a business plan, capitalizing and organizing the business, budgeting and managing cash, and implementing employee policies and practices. The book will also address dealing with partners (often your friends, at least for now). I'll also look at managing your time—the business owner's most precious resource. Finally, I will address how to handle legal issues and "back-office" functions—payroll, human resources, accounting, cash management, taxes, etc. (all the boring stuff that you don't want to think about now!)—in a cost-effective manner.

Throughout this book real-life experiences will be cited as examples (with the names changed to protect the innocent), and a couple of hypothetical start-up businesses—*TDH Accounting Services* and *Tony's Fine Italian Restaurant*—will be used to demonstrate concepts.

Technical terminology or "jargon" is explained and defined, so even the business novice can benefit from this book. A section with *Definitions of Business Jargon* is included as <u>exhibit A</u>, and any underlined terms in italics are defined there.

INTRODUCTION

Summary

The goal of this book is to prevent poor execution from killing a great business idea. The book is not a substitute for an MBA. However, it is certainly cheaper and probably more on point in detailing certain real-life issues entrepreneurs may encounter.

1

EVERYONE SAYS MY IDEA IS GREAT!

You Want to Do What?

It all starts with an idea. Family, friends, and your spouse all think the idea is great, so it must be, right?

Well, let's test it!

> **Landmine #2:** *If the idea for the business can't be stated in two to three sentences so the "average" person can understand it, it probably isn't going to work. Said another way, if the customer can't easily understand the business, it will likely fail.*

Sounds easy enough, right? Unfortunately, not everyone gets it. I have personally sat through many meetings where the management team was unable to agree on a simple, focused mission statement—really nothing more than a statement of the business idea or concept. The primary pitfall seems to be that many times managers want their business to be everything to everybody, and that just plain doesn't work.

So, KISS

No, not the rock band: "Keep it simple, stupid."

Many founders of companies have done it right. There are many excellent examples of easy-to-understand business concepts. Consider these four:

- "Premium Coffee Drinks in a Comfortable, Friendly Atmosphere"
- "Always Low Prices"
- "Fun, Low Airfares"
- "Fast Burgers, Fries & Shakes"

Each of the above should trigger the name of a successful company. It is more than quality advertising that allows people to quickly relate each concept to a company. Rather, it is everything about the company, along with its advertising, that clearly identifies it with one of the above descriptions. The point is that successful businesses, especially if they are consumer-oriented, generally have a single, clear business concept behind them.

Coffee That Tastes Good!

Think about it: how hard was it to recognize in the pre-Starbucks era that coffee served by restaurants, convenience stores, businesses, airlines, and gas stations was crappy? Even coffee available for home consumption from stores was awful.

Talk about complex business ideas: "Hmm, we need an idea for a new business. I know, let's make and serve coffee that tastes good. Let's serve our coffee in a nice place and be friendly with our customers" (a real brainstorm!).

Wow! What a complex, detailed, complicated strategy for a new business! Almost impossible to understand, right?

Quite the contrary.

Howard Schultz, credited by most as the founder of Starbucks's retail outlets, was able to satisfy our test of being able to simply and clearly describe his business concept. At the time you might have told Howard that his plan was flawed because only an idiot would pay more than fifty cents for a cup of java. However, that's not the point; our first test is very simply whether the business concept can be easily communicated and understood. There is no doubt that Howard's concept met that requirement.

Always Low Prices!
Sam Walton's "always low prices" slogan is another example of an extremely easy-to-understand business concept. Imagine Sam thinking, "I've got it; let's sell the same everyday products as other stores but sell them for less." Again, at the time you could have questioned Sam's ability to make a profit while selling at much lower prices than the competition, but that's a different test. The logistics involved in Sam making his idea successful are ancillary at this stage. The key point is the concept, which was and is singular, clear, and easy to understand.

Fun, Low-Cost Air Travel!
Southwest Airlines' goal is to make air travel fun. Tough job, right? Even more difficult, making *discounted* air travel fun—now that's truly a tall order. This simple, but seemingly impossible, concept, has allowed Southwest to grow into one of the most profitable airline companies in the world.

> *I was flying Chicago to Reno, a four-hour flight. The flight was completely full. We were nearing Reno, and the pilot came on and told us that due to thunderstorms in Reno, we were going to have to divert to Sacramento, refuel, wait for the storms to subside, and then come back to Reno. On any other airline, this would have been a total downer, causing immediate sighs, groans, and complaints, —but not on Southwest.*
>
> *Why?*

The pilots and flight attendants at Southwest get it—they have bought into and understand the company's core business: make it fun!

As soon as the announcement was made, the pilots and flight attendants started making light of the whole situation: cracking jokes about how nice the bathrooms were in Sacramento, offering free cocktails, and generally yucking up the whole situation. Their humor was neither forced nor fake; instead, it was self-deprecating and genuine, and the passengers loved it. They even stopped a passenger who was late reboarding in Sacramento, made him tell everyone where he was staying in Reno, and forced him to agree to buy all the passengers free drinks that night at his hotel bar.

When we arrived in Reno, the passengers clapped, laughed, and cheered as the pilot continued making jokes about getting lost. The people profusely thanked the flight attendants and pilots when they offloaded in Reno, **almost four hours late***!*

You can say that only skiers, drunks, and gamblers fly to Reno, so they don't care about time constraints. Maybe. There are less well-heeled and fewer business travelers on this route. However, somehow SWA has figured out that people really care more about having fun than they do about getting somewhere on time.

The other airlines think that they are in the transportation business. Pity them. The bottom line is that Southwest isn't really even in the same business as the other airlines. The other airlines are bus companies, while Southwest is an amusement park operator. Who would you rather fly?

Fast Food!

We take it for granted, but it wasn't always that way. When Ray Kroc founded McDonald's (or purchased the rights to the concept from the McDonald brothers), I believe food service was pretty much a sit-down, order, and wait affair. Ray decided that the simple concept of serving a few food items fast (something he observed on a trip to California) was the key strategy for his new business. Another basic, simple business idea easily understood by anyone—customers and employees alike.

<u>Complexity = Failure</u>

Let's compare these successful business strategies to one of my failed business start-ups. I tried to start a business that I thought would be great. It was based on a unique but somewhat tricky concept—my own, of course.

After spending about $12,000 on legal fees and preliminary marketing materials, including a website and some promotional materials, I realized that the basic offering was too complex for my customers—homeowners. Furthermore, the business's complexity made it seem like a scam, so I cut my losses and closed the business.

What was my new business concept that failed? (As you read the following, don't be surprised if it doesn't make sense—which is, of course, the point!)

My new company would buy existing houses using a "contract for deed." This would allow us to buy houses from sellers who were underwater (their mortgage loan balances exceeding their house's value), and the sellers would not have to pay off their mortgage loan at closing. My company was not going to assume the mortgage loan but would buy the property subject to the loan remaining in place. My company would not make the seller's loan payments but, instead, would send letters to the lender, offering to renegotiate the loan (with a principal reduction). If we were successful, the sellers would get out of their mortgage and walk free and clear, but if we weren't, the lender could still come after the sellers, as technically they were still the borrowers. To protect the sellers, we would offer a $10,000 indemnity, like insurance…blah, blah, blah.

If you understood the foregoing, you are probably an attorney; otherwise, no one could really understand what I was trying to do.

Compare the above almost incomprehensible explanation for my home-buying business to the other successful business concepts discussed above. The differences should be pretty obvious. My idea for buying homes using a "contract for deed" was cute and legally valid (remember, I spent a bunch on legal fees vetting it), but to the customer, it was too convoluted, too confusing, too contingent, and too hard to explain, and as a result, it failed miserably.

The Hurdles

The next test of the business idea is: Can it be done? Is it realistic?

Landmine #3: *Minimize your investment of time and money until you can determine that the things that you cannot control can get done.*

It kind of goes without saying, but there are so many times when I have seen would-be entrepreneurs spend endless time working on certain more detailed aspects of their business idea only to find themselves unable to launch, due to factors outside their control. Instead, work on things that need to get done; don't waste time and money.

I had clients who wanted to open an auto body shop. I spent a year and a half working with them, but they never seemed to get through some of the key hurdles for opening the business, like getting a lease for the space. However, they had plenty of pens and baseball caps with the name of their new business.

Here are some of the factors that can prevent the business from even getting started:
- *capital*,
- legal or regulatory hurdles,

- family or partner issues, and
- third-party agreements.

Please note that the upfront investment of both time and cash should be minimized, not eliminated. As explored further in some of the following chapters, entrepreneurs must spend time and some money to adequately plan and describe their business ideas or concepts to prospective investors or lenders.

Doing enough work to flesh out a business idea is okay. However, spending too much time on detailed policies and procedures during the planning and formation phase is not.

To start a new business, the main hurdles or obstacles standing in the way of the entrepreneur must be identified. I have identified several potential obstacles above, but each situation is different, so this is something that needs to be developed for each new business. Once the obstacles are identified, the work needed to be done to clear each one must be laid out. At that point, the focus should be almost exclusively on getting over those hurdles.

This can be hard because clearing the hurdles will not necessarily be the most fun or exciting thing. So for example, a chef wanting to start his or her own restaurant will typically want to focus on the menu and location. Important, of course; in fact, they are critical. But if getting released (freed) from a noncompete agreement with a former employer is needed, doesn't it make sense to focus on the release before getting too far down the road on the rest of the new business?

Will It Work on Paper? Is It Feasible?

The next test of the new business concept is whether it is feasible on paper. I guarantee that if it doesn't work on paper, it won't work in real life. So the idea must be reduced to writing.

Landmine #4: *If you don't have a plan, you don't really know where you are going.*

A "business plan" is nothing more than a written description of the idea and how to implement it—it documents the path ahead and how it will be followed. Many entrepreneurs try to start without a written plan. How silly is that? Even if a plan is not needed for investors or banks, isn't it just common sense to write down the idea and plans? If the only benefit is just to solidify things for the business owners, in my opinion it is still worthwhile.

Some people, even some with business experience, are intimidated when it comes to preparing a business plan. This is, of course, ridiculous. Anyone with a business concept needs to be able to reduce it to writing. The specific topics to be addressed in a business plan are listed and described in detail in chapter 2.

Entrepreneurs don't have to be accountants to prepare a plan. All that is required is a little discipline, realism, and the ability to be honest. Preparing a written plan forces entrepreneurs to think about the business in ways that they may not have in the past, which is, of course, a good thing.

It goes without saying that any investors (other than possibly family and some friends) and certainly any prospective lenders will insist on a complete business plan. Simply explaining the business idea, no matter how good it is or how passionate people are about it, will not satisfy investors or lenders. They will want a business plan.

More sophisticated investors review many business plans. Such investors may stop reviewing a plan as soon as they see any inconsistency, completely dismissing the entire concept under the theory that entrepreneurs who can't take the time to prepare a credible plan certainly won't be able to deal with all of the issues that will confront them as business _owner/managers_. (This is similar to how a misspelling on a résumé often leads to the résumé being discarded.)

How do you prepare a credible business plan? Glad you asked! Read on, as the next chapter will provide the answer.

Summary

Your business concept must be easily understood by the target customer. Things that are outside of your control—hurdles—must be addressed early in the planning process, before significant time and money are invested. You must prepare a written business plan to provide a road map for how the business idea will be converted into an operating business that makes money.

2

WHO NEEDS A BUSINESS PLAN?

The Basics

A business plan is nothing more than a written narrative describing your business concept, plans to implement, and projections of financial results. Anyone can prepare one; every business <u>*owner/ manager*</u> should prepare his or her own.

There is no right or wrong way to prepare or organize a business plan, but there are certain topics that are typically covered and should be included. Those topics include:
- executive summary;
- basic description of business;
- list of management team members and their experience;
- plan of action and timetable to launch;
- marketing and sales programs;
- competition and competitive advantages;
- real estate needs;
- employees and compensation programs;
- capital needs supported by a start-up-cost budget;
- business risks;

- accounting and administration; and
- monthly cash flow budget (operations by month for eighteen to twenty-four months).

Nondisclosure or Noncircumvention Agreements

Before addressing the business plan topics, a word here on nondisclosure or noncircumvention agreements, also referred to as *NDAs*. The issue is whether giving a business plan to someone puts that person in a position to move forward without you. If the answer is yes, people will often request that the party receiving the plan sign an NDA. The purpose of the NDA is to prevent the reader from stealing your idea.

In practice, it is very difficult to prevent someone who is unscrupulous from stealing an idea—no matter what the NDA says. Therefore, I wouldn't suggest spending endless time and money preparing and negotiating NDAs. Would I have an attorney draft an NDA that could be used multiple times? Yes, that would be prudent. Would I have people sign it and retain a copy? Yes. Would I expect to be able to recover huge sums of money from someone who signed an NDA but stole my idea anyway? No, I wouldn't.

Executive Summary

This is the first section in the plan, and it is the hardest section to write because it needs to be concise. It should be limited to one page, if at all possible, and should never be more than two pages, no matter how complex your product or how compelling your business idea.

This is also the most important section of the plan.

By way of example, think of the lost art of door-to-door sales or even telemarketing. The prospect answers the door or picks up the phone and says, "Hello." The salesperson now has seconds to say something to get that person's attention. In effect, the salesperson needs to give the prospect a "teaser," something that will pique the person's interest enough so that he or she will continue listening.

It is the same concept for the executive summary section. Its purpose is to get the reader to read on and learn more about your incredible new business. If the summary is too long, the reader will lose interest. If it's too short or doesn't give enough information, there may not be sufficient interest to read on.

Basic Description of Business

State the business idea clearly and succinctly. Add details on the location of the business, product description, target market, marketing programs, sales and pricing strategy, staffing requirements, etc. This section needs to be long enough to inform the reader regarding exactly what your plans are and what the business will look like when up and running. No need to get into the implementation or start-up issues here. This is your chance to show your vision for *what the business will be* when it is up and running.

I was recently describing a new business idea to a prospective partner—someone I had known for a while but had never really done much business with. After listening patiently for ten minutes, the listener was finally able to ask me a question: "I get it, but how do you make any money?"

Ouch! Ten minutes of explaining and I hadn't covered that basic issue; not good. The answer was on volume because the basic business was low margin, so only through multiple sales locations and high volume would the business be able to succeed. I should have stated this early on.

Make sure that the reader of your business plan is not asking a question like the one above after reading this section of your business plan.

Who Needs a Business Plan?

Management Team Members and Their Experience

The reader needs to know that the right people—the management team—have been assembled to execute the plan and manage the business. Remember **Landmine #1**: many new businesses fail not because of a bad idea but because of poor execution. This section demonstrates that your execution will be flawless.

> **Landmine #5:** *Even in today's world, investors still bet on people. As owner/managers, you must be able to demonstrate clearly that your team is well suited to make the business successful.*

This section should include what are known as "bios," not résumés. Bios are one to two paragraphs on each person, describing his or her credentials. The plan should include bios for all of the partners with emphasis on *owner/managers*, supervisors, and managers. In no circumstances should you include more than four to six bios. Make sure that the reader can ascertain from the bios who has operational experience and who has financial experience. Investors get nervous if there are no accountant/financial types watching their money. Now that the Enron and Arthur Andersen scandals are well behind us, CPAs have moved back up slightly above used-car salespeople in the rankings of the most trusted businesspeople, so there needs to be at least one financial person on the team, even if he or she is a paid outsider.

The person reviewing the plan will be looking at the experience and training of the management team to get comfortable with the fact that the team can in fact execute. If the team has absolutely no experience, training, or educational background in the chosen business field, this will be viewed as a huge negative.

Plan of Action and Timetable

In this section of your plan, simply describe the hurdles and the timetable. The hurdles should include regulatory approvals, financing or capital needs, third-party agreements, long lead-time planning issues, etc.

This section can be done on a timeline or in narrative form. A brief description of each step and the approach to each is all that is needed. Whenever giving dates, I always suggest using a range such as: "we expect to get the supplier agreements signed in one to three months, the lease agreement for our factory signed in four to six months, etc."

Marketing and Sales Programs

This section will vary significantly, depending on the business itself. Generally, in this section you should elaborate on the product, positioning (low or high end of the market), target customers, marketing programs (i.e., advertising and promotion), product pricing, and how the product will be sold.

Consider the hypothetical accounting firm, TDH Accounting Services, and how its management team might address this section.

> *Tom, Dick, and Harry were close friends from the same small town who all graduated from their state university with accounting degrees. Since they were such big buddies, they thought they might go into business together, so they formed TDH Accounting Services on their secretary of state's website.*
>
> *The men thought to categorize their services into three business lines, as follows: (1) tax compliance (preparing tax returns), (2) tax planning (helping businesses to organize, reviewing transaction documents, and providing tax advice, etc.), and (3) bookkeeping work (doing basic accounting for small businesses).*

Who Needs a Business Plan?

In the marketing and sales programs section of TDH's business plan, the partners would list these three lines of business and discuss billing rates (pricing) and profitability for each line. Guidance should be provided on the relative revenues they expect from each line of business. They could also discuss the target customers and marketing programs tailored to each.

So for tax-compliance work, the target customers might be individuals and businesses located within twenty-five miles of the TDH office. The men would leverage their local contacts and their parents' friends and business associates. Formal marketing programs might include a quarter-page print advertisement in the Sunday newspaper from November through March; radio spots on the sports talk station weekly during February through April; and finally, sponsorship of a half dozen little league baseball teams.

Competition and Competitive Advantages

The competition and how the business stacks up against competitors needs to be addressed very honestly and specifically. The reader needs to understand whether the business will compete on price, service levels, or product quality. The business plan does not have to show how the business is better in all of these areas, but it had better be able to show how it is better than the competition in some area.

Real Estate

In this section the plan needs to describe the business's real property needs and costs. This may not be an integral part of the business strategy, but it is something that can cause a premature failure. Investors know this, so it must be addressed. Many businesses end up using too much of their <u>*investment capital*</u> (cash) before they even open because they mismanage acquisitions or renovations of real property.

Landmine #6: *Approach the real estate needs of your business in a methodical and professional manner or lose a chunk of the business's <u>investment capital</u> before the business even opens. Don't try to do things on the cheap.*

People think handling real estate and construction issues is easy and can be done by anyone. Almost everyone has friends or relatives in the contracting business who they think can do the job for them. Bad idea! What can go wrong? Oh, just about everything. There are millions of examples; here's one of them:

I was recently asked by an interior designer to bid with her on a design/build project for one of her clients who wanted to renovate approximately four thousand square feet of space in a strip center. The client wanted to take the space that had been completely demolished by the landlord and build out a themed restaurant.

We came up with a proposal to do all of the design, architectural work, permitting, FFE purchasing, and construction administration and supervision for a reasonable percentage of the job costs.

The client also wanted an estimate of the total job costs and time frame to complete the build out, which was provided based on a rough estimate of the per-square-foot build-out costs. We of course wanted to provide a realistic estimate that would contain all of the job costs, including the kitchen equipment and restaurant furnishings.

Unknown to us, the client had also been meeting with several other contractors and asking them for estimates. When we provided our cost estimates, time frame, and fee proposal, the client balked because she had received another verbal cost estimate that was less than half of our estimate, along with a promise that she could be open in three months.

You might think that we would be shocked by such a large discrepancy between cost estimates, but unfortunately we had run into enough

Who Needs a Business Plan?

unscrupulous contractors to recognize this tried-and-true strategy for getting a contracting job: bid ridiculously low based on an undefined scope and then escalate the costs all along the way by saying that the original bid did not include the various required components of the job (such as architectural fees, permitting costs, equipment, upgraded flooring, or furniture, etc.).

The business owner went with the low-cost bid, so we did not get the job. Several months after having the cost estimates raised multiple times by the general contractor, the client called my interior designer friend and apologized for not believing our estimate. She said that the actual costs were already well over our estimate, and the project was not even close to being finished. I drove by the project about nine months after giving our bid, and there was still plenty of work to be done!

Never take shortcuts on construction work and face the fact that there really are no deals. If you need to plan for major renovation/construction work, interview multiple architects and contractors and consider using construction managers to supervise the process. Don't let construction cost overruns or delays kill the business before it even gets started.

In the plan, make sure to:
- describe the business's real estate needs (e.g., a storefront with approximately two thousand square feet on a major street with good visibility);
- list the status of procuring the real estate (e.g., currently deciding between two possible locations);
- show the cost of real estate (e.g., $8 to $10 per square foot lease rent, plus utilities); and
- describe expected renovation work needed and cost estimates (e.g., minor or no construction work will be needed, just purchase of display units at an estimated cost of $20,000 to $25,000).

Employees and Compensation Programs

The plan will need to include staffing needs and anticipated compensation levels. Benefit programs and their costs will also need to be described. The timing of hiring management, supervisors, and employees will need to be clearly stated. This information will be used in preparing the cash flow projections discussed in detail below.

Recruiting, hiring, and training issues need to be addressed if there are issues or concerns with getting the right people.

Most business plans that I review miss some important compensation costs. Employment taxes run approximately 8 percent of budgeted payroll costs. This is the employer's share of FICA and Medicare taxes. It must be paid, and it should be paid when you pay payroll. Nonpayment of these taxes can escalate to a criminal offense. You also need to allow for unemployment taxes and workers' compensation insurance. In total, I suggest that you budget at least 10 to 12 percent on top of your estimated wages and salary costs.

Capital Needs

In this section, you will discuss the start-up *capital* needed and the sources for the money.

How much money the business needs should be detailed in a start-up-cost budget. This is one of the most important planning tools available. This is a schedule of all of the costs and expenses that will be incurred from today through the day of the first sale. It must include any and all costs; nothing should be left out, except that nominal costs can all be captured in a "miscellaneous" line item.

> **Landmine #7:** *The start-up-cost budget needs to include a contingency line to cover unforeseen items, or your cost estimates will be too low.*

Who Needs a Business Plan?

I typically add a line item called "contingency" to cover some amount of unforeseen costs, maybe 10 percent of the total costs before the contingency line item. The amount ultimately depends on the amount of work done in preparing these cost estimates and the level of confidence that the costs are accurate.

A *sample start-up-cost budget* for one of my own past business ventures follows:

**LAS VEGAS SALES CENTER
START UP COST BUDGET**

	High	Low
Legal		
Registrations	75,000	40,000
Lease	2,500	1,500
Marketing agreements	3,500	1,500
Sales packages	20,000	10,000
Other agreements	10,000	5,000
Sales & Marketing		
Marketing materials	25,000	15,000
Sales room FF&E	50,000	30,000
Wall tour	10,000	3,000
Room build out	100,000	50,000
Broker (pre-sales)	2,000	1,000
Deposit with tour vendor	50,000	35,000
Office		
FF&E	10,000	5,000
Computers	12,000	8,000
Telephone/copier/ other	5,000	2,500
Office Supplies	2,500	1,500
Other		
Business licenses	5,000	2,500
Timeshare systems	25,000	5,000
Acccouting systems	1,500	500
Space rent/deposit (pre-sales)	50,000	30,000
Personnnel costs		
Recrutinng, hiring costs	5,000	2,500
Pre-sales payroll		
Sales mgmt	20,000	10,000
Sales training	10,000	5,000
Contracts	6,000	3,000
Working capital/start up losses	125,000	100,000
Total Start up Costs	**625,000**	**367,500**

Types of costs that may be applicable for the start-up-cost budget are as follows:
- staff recruiting, hiring, and training costs;
- staff training wages;
- lease deposit and rent before opening;
- utility hookups and preopening bills;
- construction/renovation costs, including: architectural, engineering, construction, and _FFE_ (furniture, fixtures, and equipment);
- inventory and supply purchases;
- office _FFE_, including: computers, accounting and payables system, desks, copiers, etc.;
- operating systems purchase, installation, and training;
- loan fees and costs;
- consulting, legal, accounting, and any other professional fees;
- company formation/setup and registration fees;
- merchant account fee (credit card processing); and
- working capital (to ensure that you can survive a slow start).

As far as the sources of capital for the start-up-cost budget, there are really only two primary sources of cash: (1) owner/investor contributions (called _equity_ or _investment capital_) and (2) debt (i.e., loans to the business).

The combination of equity and debt is known as the "capital structure" or "_capitalization_" of the company. People often refer to the capitalization as a ratio of debt to equity, so if a business has 60 percent debt to equity, it would mean that the bulk of the business capital is coming from the owners/investors as _equity_. A _debt-to-equity ratio_ of 150 percent would mean the opposite.

There is no perfect capitalization that applies to all businesses. Certain industries—real estate, for example—typically have higher *debt-to-equity ratios* than other industries.

Almost all businesses need some level of capital; getting it is a hurdle that must be addressed before getting too far down the road with the rest of the business. Bank loans are rather difficult to get these days. Almost any bank loan is going to require a personal guarantee and possibly additional collateral, such as a second mortgage on your house. The Small Business Administration (SBA) provides loans to certain types of small businesses, but the loans themselves still come from a bank or finance company that has a department that does SBA loans. So start with a local bank, but don't expect the bank to be falling over to lend the business money.

Any lender will be looking for a meaningful equity contribution before even considering making a loan to the business. What is meaningful? It depends, but if you need $100,000 to start your business, don't expect to get $80,000 or even $60,000 from your friendly community banker. Through SBA programs, you may be able to secure a higher *loan-to-value*, but that depends on the type of business.

The terms of any loans that the business requires, including the maturity date, need to be clearly described in this section.

Business Risks

State them and describe them without sounding defensive about the risks. Explain how those risks might be mitigated, but do not try to explain them completely away.

> *For my time-share business, the company borrowed at a floating or variable rate of interest and lent (to buyers) at a fixed rate of interest. The*

time-share business made an interest rate spread by borrowing at prime + 3 percent (around 8 percent at the time) and lending at the very high interest rate of 15 percent. The interest spread was the difference between the two interest rates—or 7 percent.

Since the business was borrowing at a variable rate and lending out at a fixed rate, if interest rates increased, the interest rate spread would be reduced. This would cut the company's profits.

I clearly delineated this "risk" in the business plan, and let the readers decide whether it was a risk worth taking or not. My opinion about the future direction of rates would have been irrelevant and would have sounded defensive, so I did not include it.

Accounting and Administration

The business plan needs to address cash management, accounting, payables, billings/receivables, payroll, HR issues, and taxes. Businesses have a number of options for handling these functions: an *owner/manager* with experience, hiring financial employees, outsourcing, etc. This section doesn't need to be too long; it just needs to make clear that there is a credible plan to address this work.

Monthly Cash Flow Budget

I suggest that the business plan include a monthly budget of cash flow (not income and expenses) for twelve to eighteen months.

One simple suggestion that can save a lot of grief in dealing with your investors and lenders is to label the columns (months) on the monthly cash flow budget as "mth. 1," "mth. 2," "mth. 3," etc. This labeling is much wiser than actually putting down the names of the months. Since often there are delays in start-up, inevitably the months will not match up.

For example, let's assume that you ignore my suggestion because it just seems a little silly. Instead, you use the actual names of the months.

Who Needs a Business Plan?

The plan is to start operations in June 2021, so that is the first month on the monthly cash flow budget. The budget assumes that the business will have three months where it loses money each month, and then after that, beginning in September 2021, the business will be "cash flowing" (making money!).

Due to unforeseen problems (maybe you didn't do a great job with identifying and dealing with the hurdles), the business start-up is delayed three months until September. Other than the three-month delay, things go pretty much exactly as planned, with losses coming in as budgeted for the first three months. You are feeling good and on top of things, but you get a call from your banker asking what's wrong with the business. Why?

This is because the banker is taking the actual results for September and October 2021 and comparing them to your original budget for those same months. Remember, in your business plan you assumed start-up in June 2021 and that you would be profitable by September and October. In effect, the banker is comparing apples to oranges, but from his or her perspective, the banker is comparing September and October 2021 budget to September and October 2021 actual. When the banker saw that the budget was for income but the actual was a loss, you got the phone call.

If you had taken my suggestion, the banker would have matched up your "mths. 1 and 2" with your actual numbers for September and October 2021, and the banker would have seen that you were right on plan, as these ended up being the first two months of operations when losses were projected.

One of the typical mistakes that new business owners make is not properly matching the timing of cash receipts with cash expenditures. I can tell you from experience that receipts come late, while the cash is flying out the door and when the new business's vendors and suppliers are demanding payment now.

New Business Landmines

Landmine #8: *Use cash flow for budgeting, not income and expenses. Make sure you watch the first couple months and get the timing of receipts and payments correct. Generally, cash will go out much quicker than you think and come in much slower.*

Let's consider TDH Accounting Services and their start-up:
The men got the funding that they needed and opened up for business.

TDH planned to bill most of its clients through the mail. TDH had done a start-up-cost budget on a net income basis—leave it to the accountants to use income, not cash flow! So for its first month's budget, TDH showed its fee income and expenses. The company showed enough income to cover its projected expenses, which were mostly payroll and rent.

Unfortunately, the bills to TDH's clients for most work performed by the accountants during the first month were not even mailed until the twenty-fifth of the month. Most payments were not received by TDH until late in the following month.

But what about the expenses? Could they be delayed until the customers' payments were received? Hardly! The payroll must be made on time, and the same was true for the rent.

TDH's first month's budget showed adequate revenues to cover expenses, but TDH's owners missed the fact that the expenses would actually be payable in cash during the first month, while the revenues would not actually be collected until month two, leaving them with an unforeseen cash deficit and hence a capital call. Mom and Dad to the rescue!

To solve this problem, you must use cash flow for budgeting, especially for a start-up business. Be realistic in your assumptions; never assume the best case.

There was a realtor I had worked with who was a pretty good realtor. She had sold a custom home or two for me when I was building

Who Needs a Business Plan?

single-family houses. I remember the fateful day when she called with the "big news" that she had secured some investment capital and was planning to purchase and renovate a house.

She asked if I would be her general contractor. I agreed.

I knew there was an investor, but I had assumed that my realtor friend would still need to secure a construction loan. Normal practice would be for me, as the general contractor, to prepare monthly "draws" (effectively, bills) that would include all of the work done during the prior month by all of the subcontractors (carpenters, painters, bricklayers, etc.) and deliveries by suppliers (lumber, carpet, appliances, etc.). The realtor would then approve the draw, and I would process it with the title company, who would cut checks to the various subcontractors and suppliers (funded by the construction loan).

When I reviewed this entire process with the realtor, she was dumbfounded. After an uncomfortable silence, I asked her what was wrong. I'll never forget her response. She said, "Loan? Why would I need a loan?" I was initially surprised but finally said, "Wow, great news! Your investor has deeper pockets than I thought, so we will be paying all the subs and suppliers with the investor's money?"

Again, the same dumbfounded look on the realtor's face, and she responded, "I don't understand. Why would I need to pay the subcontractors and suppliers monthly? Can't they just wait until I sell the house?"

I should have walked away right then, but instead I kept trying to educate and work with this person. She just thought that she could do business the way she envisioned, not the way it was actually done. Unfortunately, she ultimately declared bankruptcy and stiffed me and one of my subcontractors on his fees. In the end, I had to make good on the subcontractor's bill.

Oh, the house in question? It was still for sale almost three years later! Now that would have been one patient subcontractor to have waited three years to get paid!

So again, understand the business and be realistic about the amount and timing of expenses. Be conservative in preparing the budgets. Do not assume the best case or the worst, for that matter. Some people do two sets of numbers or even three sets—a best case, a medium case, and a worst case.

I have attached a sample monthly cash flow budget for your consideration as exhibit C.

Summary

Follow the simple rules and suggestions from this chapter and prepare your own business plan. I have attached copies of two sample business plans as exhibit B1 and exhibit B2, which you can use as a reference. Preparing the plan yourself will not only impress potential investors and lenders, but the process may also serve as a tool to help in better evaluating the plan. There is no better person to explain the plan and to sell it than the owner/manager. If assistance is needed, engage someone to review and critique the plan, but take the lead as the owner/manager!

3

A Bank Will Give Me the Money, Right?

The concept has been vetted. The business plan, including the monthly cash flow budget and a start-up-cost budget, prepared. The business now needs _capital_ to get off the ground.

My theory has always been that money will always be available to fund a great plan. My theory is probably a little naïve. Generally, unless the concept or product is absolutely, screamingly great—like the next Twitter or Facebook—it may not be that easy to get the money needed to launch. According to the movie *Social Network*, even Mark Zuckerberg (founder of Facebook) had to get the $20,000 he needed to move forward with Facebook from his wealthy college friend.

Small business start-ups are typically funded by their owners and their families, not banks or venture capitalists.

Start by looking at the _owner/manager's_ own sources of cash. Refinancing a home mortgage loan or getting a home equity line of credit are typically easy ways to get money that often can be used for any purpose. The interest rates on these loans are probably the lowest that can be obtained by the typical entrepreneur.

Credit card advances are not a great source of cash because of the high rates, but they can be used in a pinch for short time periods. Please make sure to have a plan to retire any credit card debt as soon as possible and follow through on the plan.

A note about business credit cards: there are many offers out there for "business credit cards." Please know that most or all of these offers require the business owner to *personally guarantee* the charges. This doesn't mean that you should not consider using these cards; it is just important to understand that whoever applies for and signs the credit card agreement will be personally liable.

Another option that I have not used, but did explore once, was to use a 401(k) account to fund a business start-up. There are a number of companies that can help with structuring this for an upfront fee plus ongoing annual payments. However, be advised that there are some very specific requirements regarding structuring, and as I remember, the business must be *organized* as a corporation.

Can You Lend Me...?

If the owner/managers do not have the cash and cannot get it, then what options exist?

> **Landmine #9:** *The person asking for money wears the tie; the person with the money gets to wear whatever he or she wants.*

The next step is to discuss the new business idea with friends and family. My advice is to keep things as businesslike as possible. Start by briefly mentioning the new business to a friend or family member who you think may have the financial wherewithal to fund your business. Do not oversell; put out a few feelers and see what interest they generate. Who knows—maybe your great Aunt Sophie has always wanted to be in the restaurant business!

A Bank Will Give Me the Money, Right?

Assuming someone shows some interest, offer to send the person the business plan and meet with him or her to discuss it further. Again, don't try to oversell or railroad anyone. People push back and feel that they are being "scammed" when things move too fast or when they sense that someone is trying too hard to sell them something. I realize that not selling your idea too aggressively may be difficult because at this point most entrepreneurs are really excited about their idea and have convinced themselves that it will succeed. However, remember that the idea probably took time to develop; give some time to potential investors to catch up. Show passion but don't stampede them.

I suggest meeting in a setting that is not a place where you typically would interact with that person. Maybe take him or her to lunch or breakfast. Try to create an atmosphere that is businesslike and that demonstrates your seriousness and resolve.

Network with former acquaintances in business and ask them for advice. It is easier than asking for money and sometimes yields the same result. So call your friend's dad who has had a successful career. Tell him about the plans for the new business. Explain that you are trying to get as much advice as possible from successful businesspeople (patronizing, if done correctly, is often very effective!). Offer to take him to breakfast before he leaves for work someday. He will probably be very happy to go to breakfast and will be surprised when you pay. He may surprise you by showing some interest in investing, but don't ask him for money; again, just ask for advice. Limit the breakfast to forty-five minutes to an hour, and before leaving ask him what steps he thinks you should take next and who he recommends that you speak with. He may know someone who currently works or has worked in your line of business who may be able to help with advice or money.

Banks

Go to the bank and ask for money. Don't go to a large bank; go to a small community bank. The bank probably isn't going to give you the money, but the experience of talking with a banker, seeing what questions bankers ask, and presenting the idea in a business-like and concise manner could be invaluable. Instead of asking for a loan, ask the banker under what circumstances the bank would lend money to your business.

Consider the following alternative exchanges:

Option #1   The entrepreneur says, "Now that I have shown you my business plan and answered all of your questions, will the bank lend me money to start my new business?"

Mr. Banker answers, "I'm sorry…blah, blah, blah." Mr. Banker is thinking, "Is this guy nuts?"

Option #2   The entrepreneur says, "I really appreciate the opportunity to show the bank my business plan today. Under what circumstances would the bank consider making a loan to this type of business?" Mr. Banker says, "Well, that's an interesting question. We do like to support new businesses, but generally we would be looking for _personal guarantees_ and some form of _collateral_, so we would need to see your _personal financial statements_." Mr. Banker is thinking, "I wonder whether this guy has any _net worth_ or _collateral_ that I could use to justify making a loan?'

The old saying pertains: it's not what you say; it's how you say it. In the end, it is unlikely that a bank will make a loan to a start-up. If the bank will consider it, it will typically require 35 to 50 percent _equity_ (owner/investor cash contributions to the total start-up-cost budget) and a _personal guarantee_ from a financially strong borrower. In other words, generally banks will only lend to people who don't need the money. However, establishing and maintaining relationships with the local community bank is always a good idea, and it could lead to a loan someday for expansion or another purpose.

SBA Loans

Ultimately, many new business owners find a bank that does Small Business Administration (SBA) loans, specifically Program 7a loans. The terms and conditions for an SBA loan are rather stringent. However, SBA loans can be obtained with lower levels of _equity_ than other lenders would require. Many people say that an SBA loan can be obtained with no _equity_. This is baloney; some level of cash _equity_ is typically needed, usually ranging from 10 to 25 percent, depending on the business and the _collateral_.

It goes without saying that if a bank makes your business a loan, the business will open its checking accounts there and purchase other services there. Community bankers are relationship oriented. That's the way it works. If accounts have been set up elsewhere, close them and reopen them at the bank willing to loan to the business. It's a hassle, but do it anyway.

Other Investors

There are some new and interesting ways of raising _equity capital_ on the Internet. One process is known as "equity-based crowdfunding." These websites say that they can raise _capital_ for businesses through social networking sites. It's beyond my pay grade to understand how these websites get around "Blue Sky" regulations (Securities and Exchange Commission rules regarding raising capital that are meant to prevent fraudulent operators from bilking the unsuspecting) governing raising _capital_. But in a pinch, exploring these sites further may be worthwhile. However, tread easy and make sure to consult outside legal counsel before committing to anything.

There are cases where entrepreneurs have put their ideas for a new business on social networking sites and have been able to get interest from private investors who liked their passion and business plans. This can be especially effective if the business provides some kind of social benefits, such as being "green."

Recently, I heard a radio commercial from Sam Adams Beer touting the company's willingness to lend to a start-up. The program was *Sam Adams Brewing the American Dream*. So keep your eyes and ears open for these kinds of opportunities.

Private equity, venture capital, insurance, and finance companies, as well as other types of investors, are out there for certain types of businesses and certain types of industries. It is wise to investigate how other businesses like yours were funded and by whom. Investors typically invest in certain fields, so if they have done one deal for a similar type of business, they may be interested in your plan too. Do not be afraid to contact these people directly by telephone or by trying to set up an appointment. E-mails are too easy to delete, and there is too much spam, so e-mails will probably not be effective.

Summary

Network! Talk with people, explain what you are trying to do, get their input, ask questions, and always ask what they would recommend that you do next. You never know where the money might come from, even though it probably won't come from a bank.

4

DO I NEED A COMPANY?

Generally, consult with legal counsel and a practicing CPA in making a decision on how to _organize_ the business. By _organizing_ the business, I mean determining what form of "corporate" organization to use, if any. I provide the following summary-level guidance from my personal experiences to familiarize the reader with the key issues.

The question is whether the new business will be operated as a:
1. sole proprietorship;
2. partnership;
3. limited liability company (LLC); or
4. corporation—two types for tax: C corporation (C corp) or Subchapter S corporation (S corp).

The factors that go into making this decision are liability, taxes, number of owners, flexibility of distributions, and cost of organizing.

Sole Proprietorship

This can be used for an individual starting and managing a business. It requires no formation agreements. Typically a business license is still needed. Often sole proprietorships are operated using a business name such as *Smith's Dry Cleaning* that includes the business owner's name.

Probably the biggest issue with a sole proprietorship is that it provides no protection against liability. In other words, creditors of the business can come after the owner personally for the business's liabilities because the business and the owner are one and the same. In other words, the business really is not a separate entity from the owner personally. For an entrepreneur with no personal assets (i.e., nothing to lose), this form of organization is fine; otherwise, it is not recommended.

For tax purposes, the income and expenses from the business are included on the owner's personal tax return on Form 1040 Schedule C. As such, there is no _double taxation_ (see discussion below).

Sole proprietorships are probably the least expensive form of organization. An attorney is probably not necessary to start a sole proprietorship, except maybe for an initial consultation.

A Note on the "Business" versus the "Company"

The following may be rudimentary for some, but I offer it to clarify the difference between "the company" and "the business."

For all of the other forms of business ownership (besides a sole proprietorship), a separate "person" is formed. The separate person is the company, which must be named and registered with the secretary of state (in the state where the company is formed) and the IRS. The company is owned by the _owner/managers_ and _investors_.

The company then owns and operates the business. The managers of the company manage the company and the business. The managers may or may not be owners. In this book, I use the term

Do I Need a Company?

owner/managers for a person who is both. I use the term _investor_ to refer to a person who owns the company but does not manage the business. So when I refer to the owners "owning the business," I really mean that the owners own the company that in turn owns the business. The chart titled "Relationship Company & Business," included in the next section, shows a visual of these concepts for _Tony's Fine Italian Restaurant_.

For any company, whether _organized_ as partnership, _LLC_, or corporation, there will be certain costs. The one-time cost to organize and register the company with the secretary of state varies but often can be in the range of $500. There is also an annual report that must be filed each year with the state, and that cost approximates $200 each year. The company will also need a registered agent in the state of incorporation. Registered agents typically charge $150 per year, sometimes less. If an attorney is used to handle these filings, he or she will charge fees too, ranging from several hundred dollars to a thousand dollars or more to assist with the initial _organizing_ of the company.

If there is more than one owner, it is often required and is highly recommended that you have an attorney prepare and walk you through a governing document for the company. I see many _owner/managers_ ignore the content of the governing document or proceed without one. This is an awful mistake. You should make your attorney draft and explain each section and what it means. Then you should ask questions and suggest changes for provisions that you don't like or understand. Although some in the legal profession pretend that there is, there is no one-size-fits-all when it comes to the governing document. Yours should be tailored to your business and to you and your partner's preferences. For a more detailed discussion on this topic, check out chapter 13—He's My Friend, so We'll Be Good Partners.

Finally, the company will also have to file a tax return with the IRS each year and with most states. Even though partnerships and *LLCs* don't actually pay a tax, they must file informational tax returns that effectively allocate the company's income between the owners—called partners for a partnership or <u>members</u> for an <u>LLC</u>. The cost to have the business tax return prepared and filed can range from as little as $500 to several thousand dollars, depending on the size and complexity of the business and the quality of your financial records.

Partnership

Before the relatively recent expansion of <u>limited liability companies</u>, partnerships were used often by entrepreneurs forming new businesses. There are two types of partnerships: general and limited. In general partnerships, all of the partners are general partners. In a limited partnership, there are one or more limited partners, and there must be at least one general partner.

Typically in a partnership arrangement <u>owner/managers</u> become general partners, and <u>investors</u> become limited partners.

> Bruno and Tony formed the company as a partnership and named the partnership "Tony's Italian Food, LP" (LP for limited partnership). The business owned by the partnership is named "Tony's Fine Italian Restaurant." Bruno's mother invested $25,000 in the partnership. Bruno and Tony, as <u>owner/managers</u>, will be the general partners (GPs), while Mom would be a limited partner (LP), as she is not involved in management. The three partners split ownership equally, as Mom put up the <u>equity capital</u>, and Bruno and Tony will manage the company and the business.

The following chart shows the ownership of Tony's and delineates the relationship between the <u>owner/managers</u>, <u>investor</u>, the company, and the business.

Do I Need a Company?

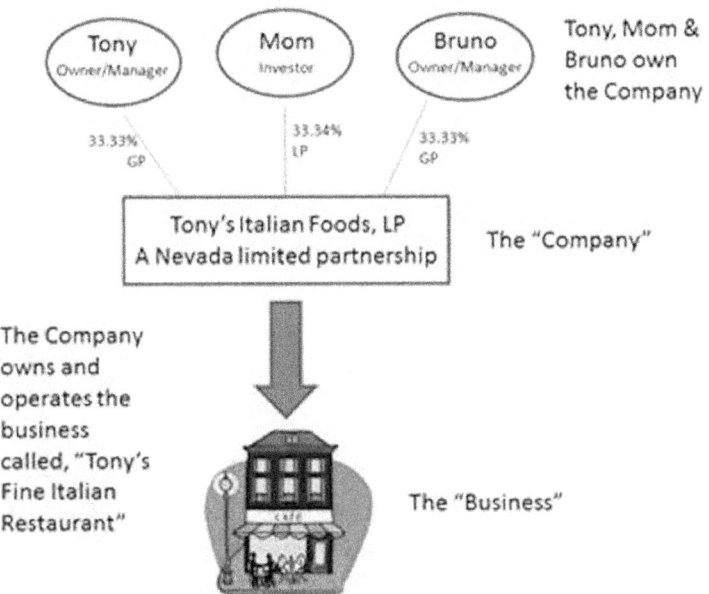

General partners are personally liable for the debts of the partnership. Limited partners are not liable for the partnership's (i.e., the company's) debts and are not involved in management.

A partnership, general or limited, is considered a "conduit" or "flow-through" entity for tax purposes. This is a fancy way of saying that the partnership does not pay taxes on its income. Oh, don't worry about the government; it still gets its money. What happens is that the income "flows through" from the partnership into the owners' personal tax returns. In effect, the owners add their share of the partnership's income to their other income on their personal tax returns.

Landmine #10: *For any type of company besides a corporation, the owners of the company pay the income taxes, whether they take any cash out of the company or not.*

This is a very difficult concept for many small business owners. If you do not understand this point, your company can incur unnecessary penalties and interest charges from the IRS and your state. In short, if the company is making money, the owners must typically make quarterly estimated tax payments. If this concept is foreign to you, get a good accountant and meet with him or her before starting the business to set up a plan to make quarterly estimated tax payments.

Limited Liability Company

LLCs have become the vehicle of choice for most new small businesses. The reason is that they provide the full liability protection that a corporation provides to all owners (called *members*), while requiring fewer corporate formalities (e.g., no corporate minutes and stock certificates) and more flexible distribution polices.

Even though the *LLC* shields its owners against liability for the *LLC's* liabilities, lenders, lessors, utility companies, credit card companies, and other vendors recognize this, so they will often ask the owners to *personally guarantee* a company debt. The guarantee allows the creditor to go after the owner for the company's liabilities.

An LLC is treated the same as a partnership for tax purposes. It is a flow-through entity, and the taxable income or loss from the LLC is allocated to the partners and then included in their personal tax returns.

An LLC can have many *members*. Every LLC has to have at least one *manager* who has certain defined authority and duties. The *manager* can be a *member* but doesn't have to be one.

LLCs provide maximum flexibility in terms of ownership percentages, contributions, and distributions.

Let's go back to TDH Accounting for an example.

TDH is organized as an LLC. The members, Tom, Dick, and Harry, decide to hire an office manager, Sally, and they want to give her a 10 percent ownership interest. This would result in the ownership interests being 30 percent for each of the men and 10 percent for Sally. Sally thanks the men for their kind ownership grant but explains that she has a burning need for $3,000 in cash as soon as she can get it.

The men decide that rather than raising Sally's salary or paying her a $3,000 bonus, it would be better to make a special distribution of cash flow to her. The men decide that they will leave the ownership percentages as agreed but provide in the <u>operating agreement</u> that the first $3,000 in cash distributions (from cash flow) will be made to Sally. After that, the next $27,000 in distributions will be made to Tom, Dick, and Harry, which will bring the total of $30,000 in distributions back into the proper ownership shares (as Sally would have $3,000 of a total of $30,000 in distributions, equaling her 10 percent ownership share). Then distributions can go back to being made in accordance with the ownership shares.

<u>LLC</u>s allow partners to create these types of special distribution schedules, but corporations do not. In corporations, distributions (called dividends) must generally be paid out based on relative ownership.

Corporations

Corporations are the most formal and rigid form of organization. They offer full liability protection for all owners, but they are also taxpayers, which can possibly result in <u>double taxation</u>.

Corporations file annual income tax returns and pay income taxes to the federal and state government. Corporations that file and pay taxes are often called <u>C corps</u>. The term <u>double taxation</u> applies to C corps because the C corp pays taxes on its income, and then the owners of the C corp pay taxes on dividends that they receive from the corporation! So, in effect, taxes are paid on the same income twice. Given this double taxation, most small businesses do not choose to be a C corp.

There is a significant exception to this rule that allows many small business owners to consider a corporate form of <u>organizing</u>. This exception is called a Subchapter S corporation or <u>S corp</u>. An S corp is an IRS election that must be made right after the corporation is formed and that allows a corporation to be treated like a partnership for taxes, so there is no <u>double taxation</u>.

However, for a company to be an S corp, its owners must all be real people, not other companies. I have seen this simple point missed by many small businesspeople and their tax advisors.

There is another reason, besides avoiding <u>double taxation</u>, that many small business owners *organize* as S corps: after paying the <u>owner/manager</u> a reasonable salary, the company does not have to pay self-employment taxes on any dividends. This can save over 15 percent on a portion of the business's income. The exact amount depends on the "reasonable salary" amount and the social security wage base, but annual savings could easily be in the range of $5,000 or more.

In summary, a corporation is a legal form of organizing. A corporation can be either a C corp or an S corp, which refers to its tax status only; either way, it is legally still a corporation.

Tax Rates

Changes in tax rates may impact the business form of your organization. Corporations have their own separate tax rates, which are not the same as the individual tax rates. There is significant discussion about lowering the corporate tax rate in the United States and closing loopholes (loopholes are just for the big companies anyway, not for the little guys, so I say close away!). The corporate rate now is 35 percent, and dividends are taxed from 0 to 20 percent (depending on the tax bracket). The top individual rate is

DO I NEED A COMPANY?

39.6 percent, plus Obamacare's 3.8 percent surtax on unearned income and the .9 percent Medicare add-on tax.

If corporate rates are lowered and individual rates continue to increase, small business owners must consider converting to corporate taxpayers. Currently, any *LLC* can convert to a corporate taxpayer. I have already done this for one of my businesses.

Landmine #11: *Watch for upcoming changes in the tax code. Generally, personal and corporate rates are pretty similar now. However, there is significant pressure to reduce corporate rates in connection with cutting loopholes and increasing personal rates. This may create a situation where it is advantageous to use a corporate entity for tax purposes.*

Comparison of Corporate Forms chart below provides a summary of many of the concepts reviewed in this chapter.

Comparison of Corporate Forms

	Sole Proprietor	Ltd or Gen'l Partnership	LLC	C-corp	S-corp
Owners are called?	Owner	Partners	Members	Stockholders	Stockholders
Manager is called?	Manager	General Partner	Manager	President	President
Cost to form and maintain annually?	No	Yes	Yes	Yes	Yes
Name of governing document?	None	Partnership Agreement	Operating Agreement	Bylaws and Stockholders Agreement	Bylaws and Stockholders Agreement
Annual meeting and minutes required?	No	No	No	Yes	Yes
Owner's protected from liability?	No	LP's = Yes GP's = No	Yes	Yes	Yes
Income tax return?	Form 1040 Schedule C	Form 1065	Form 1065	Form 1120	Form 1120S
Pays income taxes?	No Owners Pay	No Owners Pay	No Owners Pay	Yes	No Owners Pay
Flexible distributions?	NA	Yes	Yes	No	No

New Business Landmines

Liability Protection

So you have slogged through this chapter and its legal and tax consequences, and you have decided that you need and want liability protection. Great—but don't bother unless you are going to treat the company as separate from yourself. Let me explain by way of an example.

A new client comes to me for my firm to handle his "back-office work" and file his taxes. He has an existing LLC that he formed a couple years ago at a cost of a couple thousand dollars, as he used an attorney to do all of the organizing work.

To get a handle on his business, I ask for three to four months' bank statements. I review the following statement.

Do I Need a Company?

After reviewing this statement, I am able to give the prospective client a quote for providing accounting, payroll, and tax services. However, I also feel compelled to tell the client that he wasted his money organizing the LLC.

Why would I say that? The LLC was in fact properly formed; it had a comprehensive governing document. The filings with the secretary of state's office were current, so what's the issue?

The issue is that the owner was undercutting the separateness of the LLC from himself by using the LLC's bank account as a personal piggy bank. When the owner charges his morning coffee, his lunch at Burger King and Subway, and his evening cocktails at the local pub and then takes cash advances at the local casino, all from the business's bank account, any plaintiff's attorney suing the business will be able to argue that the owner is personally responsible for the business's liabilities, as the owner and the business are one. They are not really separate entities, as the owner treats the LLC's assets as his own personal assets. My prospective client, in effect, had created a pathway for creditors to get to his personal assets.

The point is that if you are going to go through the trouble and cost to form a company to limit your personal liability and protect your personal assets, you must treat the company and its assets as separate from your own. You personally pay for your personal expenses, and the company only pays for expenses that are truly business expenses. The IRS says that the only expenses that are ordinary and necessary to running your business are business expenses. If you adhere to this standard, you will be fine.

Summary

Although an S corp can provide some possible tax savings related to self-employment taxes after paying the _owner/manager_ a reasonable salary, a limited liability company provides tremendous flexibility in structuring and managing the company. An LLC also provides flow-through tax benefits and fewer corporate formalities. Generally, as mentioned above, companies can always convert from "flow-through' entities into tax-paying entities.

5

BUDGETS ARE OVERRATED!

I remember that when I finally left public accounting after nine years, I was having a difficult time making the transition into the "real world" of business. One day, my boss, who was also a great friend, got so frustrated with me getting bogged down in minutia that he screamed,

"*Grottke, don't you get it? It's all about getting the cash!*"

The boss was, of course, right. His outburst had a lasting impact on me. Business is about making money—cash. Sorry, but in the end, that's what it is about. All of the other nice things that can be done through a business—like sponsoring the local little league team, having nice employee perks, treating employees like human beings instead of chattel, holding United Way fund-raisers, giving to local charities, or employing your own offspring—can only happen if the business makes money. No money, no business.

Landmine #12: *Don't lose sight of this one fact: the most important thing in business is cash.*

Big public companies are sitting on billions of dollars in cash. Why? It gives them power and security. They know that when cash is short, no one can get it. Companies hoard cash today because it gives them the insurance that they need in an increasingly volatile world. They want assurance that in a pinch they can sustain themselves and their business. In other words, they want to survive! Primeval, isn't it!

As an entrepreneur, you will probably not have huge hoards of cash. However, your business needs to act just like the big boys by trying to build up cash reserves. There is no other insurance policy for your new business.

At the outset the business will be living on the edge—from week to week. The new business needs to budget, plan, and manage its cash, every week. Some weeks, one vendor may get paid, while two other vendors will have to wait. Make sure the money comes to vendors when promised, or they will never trust your statements again. Vendors never like late payments, but they can live with customers who do what they say and who communicate with them.

Generally, payroll must be paid on time, so payroll can only be reduced by cutting head count, reducing wages/salaries, or reducing hours worked. However, most states do not require that payroll be paid on the last day of the pay period. Some states allow payroll to be paid up to two weeks after the payroll period ends. In Illinois, for example, for a semimonthly payroll, payroll can be paid up to thirteen days after the end of the pay period. So if the pay period runs from the first through the fifteenth, the paychecks don't have to go out until the twenty-eighth, thirteen days later. The key is to make sure that your employees understand exactly how your payroll policies work.

I suggest using "rolling twelve-week cash forecasts." These are, very simply, twelve-week budgets. As each week ends, add a new week's budget twelve weeks out (at the end), so you always have approximately four months of cash flow projections. Honestly, I can't

Budgets Are Overrated!

see how anyone can manage a start-up without a rolling twelve-week cash forecast or something similar. Let's consider an example from *Tony's Fine Italian*:

Before opening their doors, Tony and Bruno sat down and projected revenues and all of their cash expenditures by week for the first twelve weeks. Things looked pretty tight, but in their start-up-cost budget, Bruno had included cash operating losses for the first eight weeks, so the business would have <u>working capital</u> (i.e., cash) set aside to fund projected weekly deficits.

After the first six weeks, things had pretty much gone according to the rolling twelve-week cash forecast. The business was growing slowly but in accordance with plan, so Bruno and Tony were feeling confident that they could make it.

The next week, when Bruno and Tony sat down, Tony explained that he wanted to take the restaurant to a higher level and try to get a Wine Spectator Award. Tony explained that this would require a significant expansion of the wine list to over three hundred selections and a minimum of six hundred to eight hundred bottles. Their wine distributor thought that it might cost approximately $20,000 to build up the wine inventory.

Rather than telling Tony that he is nuts and that his deep-fried pasta dishes don't really need to be matched with a $125 bottle of Brunello (a $15 Chianti being more than adequate!), Bruno suggests that they jointly review the rolling twelve-week cash forecast. Tony reluctantly agrees because he knows that adding $20,000 to inventory now cannot be covered by the projected cash flows. After some discussion of the fact that there is no cash to fund this endeavor, Tony agrees to revisit the idea later.

This is how the rolling twelve-week cash forecast can and should be used to guide and control spending. It is used to answer the question "Can we afford this cost now?" (Too bad our friends in Washington, DC, weren't put on rolling twelve-week cash forecasts years ago.)

Sometimes the forecast can point out more serious problems. For example, we can't make all of our scheduled payments for next week! Hmmm. Now what? Change something, delay something, defer an order, hold the rent check, call a couple vendors and tell them that their check is going to be a week late—do something. This is called managing your cash and managing your business. The alternative is to let your business manage you—run you out of money, so you have to go back to your investors, or, worse, to the bank.

A sample rolling twelve-week cash forecast is included as <u>exhibit D</u>. Please note that not every week is the same. Payroll hits on different weeks and comes from the hours-worked summary. Rent, utilities, and certain other charges are paid only once per month. Finally, please note that the cash balance is rolled forward from week to week, based on each week's net cash flow forecast.

Every start-up should have all of the following budgets:
- start-up-cost budget;
- monthly cash flow budget (for twelve to eighteen months); and
- rolling twelve-week cash forecast.

The first two are part of the business plan and were discussed in greater detail in chapter 2. The rolling twelve-week cash forecast is what you use week-to-week to manage your business.

In the end, budgets are tools for managing the business and for monitoring its performance.

Summary

Follow the cash, and you probably can't get too far off-track. Use a rolling twelve-week cash forecast to monitor and manage all of your receipts and payments. Before you commit to any new expenditures, make sure that they are reflected in the cash forecast, and that the business has adequate cash resources to cover them.

6

What's SEO, a New Sports Drink?

Marketing starts with the Internet. These days marketing and the Internet are almost synonymous. Not having a web presence can make people wonder about your credibility. The Internet provides a platform to do many different marketing activities and can be as dynamic or basic as the <u>owner/manager</u> decides.

Buried in the Trees
However, just creating a website accomplishes little in terms of marketing unless there is a way to drive traffic to it.

> *I have a friend who loves writing political and social commentaries and sending them to family and friends to digest, but who is not real Internet savvy.*
>
> *Recently, the friend asked me to set up a website for him. When I asked him why, he responded that he had read about people who posted their thoughts and ideas (i.e., blogged) extensively and had developed significant followings on the Internet. He was hoping to do the same with his commentaries on his new website.*
>
> *I explained that we could easily set up a website for him, and I let him know what the cost would be, which was minimal. I then offered*

that just having a website would not mean that anyone would read or even know about his commentaries being posted there. My friend seemed surprised, and I could see that he didn't really understand. I later sent the following e-mail in an effort to explain further:

Bill, we can easily set up a website, and I can have one of my people post your commentaries on the site in chronological order or arranged any way that you like. The real issue (which we discussed briefly the other night) is that once the site is set up and populated with your commentaries, how is anyone going to know that they are there? In other words, do you want us to explore alternatives for driving traffic to the site or just have it available to family and friends?

Trying to drive people to your website is generally referred to as "<u>search engine optimization</u>" or <u>SEO</u>, and it is a rather complex and tricky business. The cost to optimize can vary widely, depending on how aggressive you want to be in getting people to the site. In the absence of an optimization program, posting your commentaries on the web is no different from nailing them to a tree in the middle of the woods. Bill, said another way, without optimizing, no one will ever see your commentaries unless they just happen to stumble onto them by accident!

The critical business decision is whether customers need to be generated from the Internet. The decision is best made before creating the business website because the entire website design is different for a simple, informational website versus a website set up to generate customers. If the business starts with the informational website and then later decides to change to a website for marketing purposes, the informational website will likely have to be completely redone.

So you must decide very early on whether <u>SEO</u> is going to be an important part of your marketing program or not.

What's SEO, a New Sports Drink?

An Internet Brochure

If your business is not trying to generate customers from the Internet but is really only using the website as an informational tool (i.e., a brochure), *optimization* is not warranted.

> Bruno and Tony from Tony's Fine Italian restaurant never really expected to generate customers from the web. However, they felt they needed a web presence so that people who were thinking about coming in to dine could get driving directions, hours of operation, or look at their menu and prices. As such, they wanted to create a nice-looking site to provide the information that they felt their customers might be looking to find.
>
> Bruno decided to set up the website himself. To start, he knew he needed a name for the website. He was able to secure his first choice for a domain name, www.tonysfineitalian.com, for about twelve dollars. Using the relatively simple website design tools from the domain name provider, Bruno felt that he could select a template (for the format) and could create a serviceable website. The cost for the small-size site that he was looking at was about $130 a year. He also noticed that the provider had a customer service line where he could get help. However, right when Bruno was starting to get comfortable with the whole concept, he realized that something was missing—the content!
>
> Oops! Bruno called Tony to see if he had finished the menu, and he asked Tony for help coming up with the marketing message for the website. What should the message be to their customers? What differentiates Tony's from Uncle Guido's Restaurant (across town), other Italian restaurants, or any other restaurant, for that matter? Why would someone want to dine at Tony's? Is it price? Atmosphere? Quality of the food? Or service?

We'll call all of this the marketing message. The delivery of the marketing message can be a little different on the web, but you still need to know what the message is before completing the website. Once the message is known, the website content can be laid out fairly easily. As discussed in chapter 1, the business concept must be easily understood by the customer. In developing the marketing message, the goal is to convey this simple concept clearly. There is more on the marketing message in the next chapter.

Bruno and Tony decided that what differentiates them—sets them apart—is that Tony's Fine Italian will serve reasonably priced, down-home, original Italian recipes from the old country (from Tony's grandmother). The food will be served family style in large bowls for the entire table to share in a causal and comfortable setting. With this basic message, Bruno was able to craft the home page and other areas of the website.

Bruno did a nice home page with the marketing message surrounded by pictures of Tony's grandmother and entire extended family—kind of a nostalgic twist. Bruno also inserted the reservations policy and hours of operation on the home page, along with their phone number.

Bruno then added the following web pages:

- *"Menu," which Tony had just completed;*
- *"Driving Directions," showing the location of the restaurant on a map and linking to MapQuest for driving directions from any location that their customers might input;*
- *"About Us," to give a little background on Bruno and Tony and their vision for the restaurant;*
- *"Privacy Policy," that he ripped off from another website; and*
- *"Contact Us," for anyone wanting to contact Bruno or Tony about employment or to sell them tomato paste or anything else, for that matter.*

Bruno completed the entire site in four hours once he had the marketing message ironed out with Tony.

Go ahead and take a look at the site when you get a chance. Again, it's at www.tonysfineitalian.com. Yes, it's really there; take a look! It's nothing special, but the entire site was done in four hours and cost nothing more than the fees mentioned above.

What about e-mail addresses?

Bruno found that for the basic annual fee he can set up ten free e-mail addresses, so he sets up bruno@tonysfineitalian.com and tony@tonysfineitalian.com.

Search Engine Optimization

The decision not to optimize probably made sense for Bruno and Tony.

> **Landmine #13:** *The decision to <u>optimize</u> is critically important. If you decide to optimize, interview multiple firms and make sure that your financial commitments are tied to results before entering into any agreements.*

What about a business like TDH Accounting that is interested in generating customers online?

Tom, Dick, and Harry felt that they needed to have a prominent web presence to generate customers. Dick had read somewhere that almost half of the people looking for tax preparation help went to the Internet and Googled "tax returns," "help with taxes," or similar queries, often coupled with the name of the city or town where the person lived. Furthermore, he read that businesspeople looking for tax and bookkeeping assistance were even more likely to use the Internet to find help.

Harry confirmed that he had read the same things as Dick, and he added that he had also heard that when people land on a website, they spend three to five seconds deciding whether to keep looking at it or move on. Harry accurately concluded that the web home page for TDH Accounting, where people will land when they first get to the website, needs to be simple and must concisely convey their basic marketing message.

New Business Landmines

When they Googled tax accounting in Centerville (their business location), they saw that first a list of paid advertisers appeared. These were mostly the names of the largest accounting firms in the state, even though none had an office within ten miles of Centerville. This paid advertiser list was followed by a list of websites with a number of larger accounting firms listed first, again many of which were not local at all. Only at the bottom of the first page of the website listings were any of the smaller, local firms, including Thelma & Louise's Cut-Rate Accounting. Tom wondered out loud how TDH could ever come up in front of some of these other larger firms?

Out of curiosity, they clicked on Thelma & Louise's website. "Wow!—not very professional" was their first reaction. It seemed that ol' T & L had designed a splashy, attention-getting site: bright colors and "pop-ups" with cut-rate pricing specials; offers for "free consultations"; teaser rates for the first three months of bookkeeping services. It was all there and laid out in a format that allowed the viewer to quickly ascertain that Thelma & Louise would do the accounting work for cheap, consistent with the name "Cut-Rate Accounting." Harry wondered whether TDH should try to shed its more professional image to compete on price.

Given the importance of the web to their marketing efforts, the men decided to get some outside help. They set up meetings with three firms that specialized in website design, SEO, and marketing. They weren't sure that they wanted to spend the money to engage any of these firms, but Tom felt that they should at least advance their knowledge of the options by meeting with these companies.

Tom was right; they learned a lot, including the following:
- Website optimization is about how to get your website listed on the first page when someone does a web search using certain key words.
- There are two ways your website can come up in response to a search. The first way your site can come up is in the list of paid

WHAT'S SEO, A NEW SPORTS DRINK?

advertisers because you are one, which by definition costs money. This list is usually segregated from the "organic" or unpaid list of websites that come up in response to a search.

- *People often tend to overlook the paid advertisers, which are often segregated from the organic or unpaid search results, and focus on the organic listings.*
- *To have your website come up prominently in the organic listings requires <u>optimization</u>. The exact way optimization works is somewhat mysterious and varies from search engine to search engine. This appears to be by design because if the large search engines made the optimization methods eminently clear, then everyone would know exactly how to optimize. Obviously, this would not be beneficial to the search engine companies because they sell "optimization services" that would be irrelevant if everyone already knew how to optimize on their own.*
- *Just because your website comes up once in response to a search as, say, the fourth site listed, doesn't mean that it will continue to come up the fourth time that same search is performed. In other words, the parameters that the search engines use change from search to search. Again, this is probably to ensure that people can't decipher the exact optimization pathways.*
- *The more unique the product or service being offered, the easier it is to optimize because fewer websites are competing to come up in response to the search.*
- *Important factors in determining whether your website will come up high on the list include the design of the website, number of times that your website is accessed, use of videos, and the use of key words, along with, of course, paying the search engine company to optimize your site.*
- *Numerous companies and individuals will tell you they can optimize your site for a fee, some legitimate and some maybe not so.*

After the meetings with the marketing firms, Tom, Dick, and Harry had a meeting to determine how to proceed. All three firms were preparing proposals for TDH to develop a logo and marketing message, design a website and other written collateral materials, and perform optimization for the website. No definitive cost estimates were provided at the initial meetings, but Tom felt that the fee estimates would be approximately $20,000 to $30,000 up front, and that monthly optimization fees would be in the $2,000 range. After lengthy discussions, the men decided to review the proposals when received and to pick the best one. They felt that since they were all accountant/financial types they needed professional help with the marketing. The boys agreed that it was a pretty big investment—bigger than they had contemplated in their business plan and start-up-cost budget—but that since the web was expected to be their main source of clients, it was worthwhile.

Social Media

Using social media is all the rage today because many small business people think it is a form of free advertising. It really isn't.

In short, social media is about providing valuable content to readers. To be valuable in today's world, it must be concise and meaningful. To gain a following on social media, you must provide recurring valuable content. The time commitment to do this is large, so the cost is more about time than money, but there is a cost.

Direct advertising on social media is becoming more commonplace, but it costs money, and its effectiveness is still somewhat unclear. On the other hand, providing content can establish you and your business as experts that someone may contact at some point for assistance.

Internet Discount Programs

Groupon, Living Social, Restaurant.com, and other Internet-based discount offers can also be valuable marketing tools, especially to get customers to buy an initial trial of your product or service. Generally, the business itself will break even or lose money on these offers, but the point is to create awareness and trials, not make a huge profit on the offer. Be careful not to underestimate the possible response to one of these offers; it can be huge.

Summary

All businesses must have a website. A basic website can be set up by the owner/manager with minimal investment of money using a web template. It's okay to start out with a simple, informational website even though the owner/manager knows that the website will need to be redone later to facilitate SEO.

7

Field of Dreams, or If I Build It, They Will Come

No customers, no sales. The business gets customers through marketing. Very few new businesses are successful without some kind of marketing program. Generally, just opening a store or offering a product or service without marketing leads to failure. Hence, most new businesses need a marketing plan.

Who Are You?

A successful marketing plan must start with a clear identity for the business and the product or service being offered.

Every business needs a corporate identity—a name and logo.

One key point in picking a company name is that the business needs a name that has not already been registered with the state. This can be difficult given the large number of businesses that exist. One way around this is to have the legal, registered business name be an acronym and then register a d/b/a (doing business as) name. So for example, I once registered a business as ERV, LLC (the legal name), with a d/b/a (doing business as) name of Elite Retreat Vacations (the operating business name).

Field of Dreams, or If I Build It, They Will Come

I also recommend checking the desired business name on the Internet to see what other companies might be operating under the same name in the locations where you will be operating. If there are other businesses using the same or a similar name, see if they are in the same business and located in the same market area. If they are, pick another name. Not doing so can lead to major trouble down the road, such as in the following example.

I was a minority owner in a time-share start-up based in Lake Tahoe. Even though the managing partner lived in the Lake Tahoe/Reno area, he picked the company name Legacy Resorts. This name had to be changed because a large casino hotel had just opened in Reno (thirty-five miles away) as the Silver Legacy Resort. Same industry, hospitality, and geographic area, and therefore, a name we really couldn't use! After the owners of the Silver Legacy threatened us, we had to change our name, which meant changing the website, letterhead, envelopes, corporate policy manuals, marketing brochures, sales literature, etc.

On the other hand, when researching the company name Elite Retreat Vacations, I found a company on the Internet operating as Elite Retreat that made and sold cushy dog cages. I did not think that both companies using the same name would be a problem, and it wasn't.

A logo can be very important, but that doesn't necessarily mean that you have to spend a fortune designing one. Logos can be designed using any one of the logo design software packages available on the Internet for around fifty dollars.

Many <u>owner/managers</u> spend a significant amount of money and time on names and logos. This is usually unnecessary, in my opinion.

The business name can be the same or different than the company name. If using a d/b/a, usually the business name is the d/b/a.

Bruno and Tony were surprised to find that Tony's Fine Italian Restaurant, LP, was already registered with the state. Upon further investigation, they found that the company with that name was defunct and was not in good standing (because it had not filed an annual report with the state and had not paid the two-hundred-dollar annual report filing fee). Bruno checked on the Internet and could not find anyone using the name with a current operating business.

Considering their findings, Bruno and Tony decided it was probably okay to use the name as planned for the restaurant, but they would register the company name as Tony's Italian Foods, LP, with a d/b/a of Tony's Fine Italian Restaurant.

Message—What are you trying to say?

Everything must flow from the marketing message. It is important that the message provide customers with the following things:

1. Company or product name recognition. Sometimes a tagline or catch phrase can be used to help people remember your message. For my new firm, I use "Go QBO" at the end of our advertisements for "**Q**uality **B**ack **O**ffice."
2. Product description.
3. Reasons to buy:
   a. Low price? This reason is great for any commodity-type product or service, such as office supplies.
   b. Better quality? Use only if your product offers superior quality, like Starbucks coffees and teas.
   c. Easier to use? This selling point is great for technology-related products, such as a certain computer (e.g., the iPad).
   d. Faster results? Again, this reason can only be employed if the product or service satisfies the test of being faster, like 4G for smartphones.
4. How and where to get the product or learn more.

Field of Dreams, or If I Build It, They Will Come

The message must be clear, easily understood, and not too complex.

Target—Aim at Whom?
Every <u>owner/manager</u> must have an answer to this question before considering any form of advertising or promotion. The target must be known.

> **Landmine #14:** *Make sure you are advertising to people who may be interested in your product.*

Sometimes, it's easy to tell what kind of people watch a television show simply by watching the commercials. When you are watching a sporting event, the commercials will often be for pickup trucks, beer, and shaving cream (gee, who is being targeted?). When you are watching a child's show, the commercials will be for video games, toys, animated movies, and bicycles.

Marketing Mix
The <u>owner/manager</u> must select the combination of advertising media and promotional programs that can put the business's message in front of the target. This combination is referred to as the <u>marketing mix</u>.

Different marketing media offer different results. For instance:
- Billboards drive name recognition (how much can you really read on a billboard while driving sixty-five miles per hour and talking on the phone?).
- Newspapers come out daily or weekly and are generally used to communicate time-sensitive sales or promotional information (e.g., this weekend, get 15 percent off all purchases).

- Couponing gives an incentive for someone to try the product or service (e.g., buy this and get one free).
- Radio and television provide broad exposure (e.g., Master Lock used to spend its entire annual marketing budget on one Super Bowl commercial just for the millions of people who would see it).
- Magazines come out monthly or even quarterly and offer a chance to provide more detailed product information that will be viewed by customers over a period of time.
- Public relations is a very effective, inexpensive form of advertising (e.g., a sunglass manufacturer may send a pair of its new sunglasses to local celebrities or newspaper writers asking them to try out the new product in the hopes that the celebrity may be seen in them or that the writer may write about them).
- Direct mail represents a "shotgun" approach to advertising but can be partly focused by targeting certain zip codes or mailing lists with the desirable demographics (e.g., BMW may target a year-end sale brochure to AMEX cardholders).
- Telemarketing has become more difficult with the advent of "do-not-call" lists by the federal and various state governments. However, there are still certain products that can be sold effectively over the telephone.
- For the right kind of business, a Groupon or similar offer can create significant awareness and trial.
- Sponsorships are another effective way to promote your business among a targeted group of consumers (e.g., a local insurance agent buys a billboard at the local little league park).
- An effective Internet presence can create both a tool for communicating information about your product or service

(a quality website) and creating product awareness through _search engine optimization_ (SEO).
- Spam blasts can be conducted through companies that specialize in this activity. These companies will not give you the e-mail addresses, for obvious reasons. Instead, they will e-mail your message to their lists and will charge you based on the number of e-mail addresses that they say will receive the e-mail. The problem is that you have no way of knowing how many e-mails really went out and whether the e-mail addresses are even valid.

Choosing the Marketing Mix

It is difficult for me to recommend any one of these promotional/advertising forms over another without knowing the specific business. I can say that the costs range dramatically from one approach to another.

I recommend that the _owner/managers_ meet with different advertisers and marketing organizations and discuss the options. Remember, each of these companies will be "selling." Consequently, the owner/manager must be skeptical of all claims of potential results from any advertising program. Only through comparison shopping and discussing options with as many people as possible can you achieve the optimum results.

Generally newspaper print ads are very expensive, typically with limited success (responses). Take a look at your local newspaper; there will most likely be car and real estate ads! There may also be grocery, department store, and home store flyers, especially on Sundays. Typically there are not a lot of service ads or small business advertisements in the newspaper, and there's a reason for that. Small businesses watch their money closely and need to see more definitive results than newspaper ads typically deliver.

Magazine advertising is more focused, as ads can be placed in magazines that are read by the target audience. For example, I advertised my bank consulting service firm in magazines produced and distributed by certain bankers' associations. Zero results were achieved from these advertisements that cost me several thousand dollars for a quarter-page advertisement for three to four months.

Direct mail is also rather expensive, but the cost varies, depending on what you send out. A glossy postcard mailing can easily cost one dollar per piece with a response rate for a well-designed offer of 1 to 2 percent being normal. People are inundated with junk mail these days, most of which gets pushed into the recycle bin without even being looked at. As noted above, mailings can be directed to certain zip codes or sent out to purchased mailing lists, which may slightly improve results.

Cable television rates are surprisingly low, but you need to produce a commercial to access this option. There are companies that can and will produce commercials and then will purchase the ad slots. One option is a low-quality "infomercial," in which the owner/manager goes on television to sell his or her own product or service, like the plaintiff lawyer ads on late-night cable. This can cost as little as $10,000 to $20,000 for a low-quality production and $2,000 to $4,000 per month to run the ads in enough spots to have an impact. After three to four months a determination can be made as to whether the advertising is effective. A decision can then be made whether to continue running the commercial or not, but the production costs are obviously sunk (gone).

More elaborate television advertisements obviously cost considerably more.

Radio is similar. You need to produce a radio spot and then buy airtime. The difference is that low production quality is generally not as much of an issue because there is no visual aspect.

Field of Dreams, or If I Build It, They Will Come

As an _owner/manager_, you can do a radio commercial at a fairly low cost. Many radio stations will produce the commercial for you as long as you commit to a minimum period of advertising, often ranging from three to six months. Costs vary widely, depending upon the market and the radio station, but generally can range from $3,000 to $12,000 per month. Generally, a few radio ads are not effective because most people need to hear a radio commercial at least several times before taking action. My personal experience is that you need to run twenty to twenty-five commercials on radio per week for at least three months to have any real impact.

Networking, word-of-mouth, and working existing relationships are great marketing strategies, assuming they're an option.

My brother Tom worked as a consultant for three large accounting firms for almost twenty years. For all three firms, he ran a consulting business targeted at a specific industry. He called me one day and let me know that he was having problems with some of his partners. He told me that he was considering going to work for yet another firm.

I suggested that it was time for him to come over to the "light" and become an entrepreneur. My reasoning was that Tom was the business—he was well-known among the industry players in his geographic market area. It was obvious to me that people were hiring Tom, not his employer, and when Tom was on his own, they would continue to hire him.

As it turned out, this was pretty good advice. Tom is on his own now with almost a half dozen employees and with his revenues growing every year.

Tom markets (in this case, sells consulting projects) because he has existing relationships, and he stays active in his industry by giving speeches, writing articles, attending outings, and generally networking with decision makers.

I could write an entire book on telemarketing but will spare you the trials and tribulations. Suffice it to say that this is never going to be a low-cost marketing program. There are lead costs, physical space and equipment costs, postage costs, employee costs, and numerous issues (not exactly the highest quality people work as telemarketers; in other words, get your sexual harassment policy tuned up and in place—see chapter 11—before you open your new telemarketing center). In addition, there are significant and ongoing regulatory compliance costs (dealing with the do-not-call lists). Telemarketing is a last-resort option for marketing your business. Proceed at your own risk and with due caution.

The Internet and *SEO* that were discussed in the previous chapter are a critical part of any marketing plan.

Keep Score

Regardless what marketing mix is ultimately selected, the *owner/manager* must keep track of each program's effectiveness.

One of my brother-in-law's favorite sayings is: "Half of all my marketing works—I just don't know what half." This statement is true of so many companies today, both large and small. A small business doesn't have the luxury to spend marketing dollars and not know the result. Regardless of what marketing media is selected, the owner/manager must spend the time to track each program's success.

> **Landmine #15:** *Make sure that you put in proper metrics for measuring your marketing expense versus your results.*

Make sure to ask people when they order where they heard about the company. Keep track of the answers. Compare the source of each order to the applicable advertising program.

Field of Dreams, or If I Build It, They Will Come

If coupons are used, make sure to keep track of the cost of the coupon and how many were redeemed to see if the offer cost the business money or made it money. Don't fool yourself by relying on the "marketing is an investment" philosophy. When in a start-up mode, there is no time to think five years down the road! Marketing programs must work today, not tomorrow.

With a little bit of planning and a basic understanding of what you are trying to accomplish, all marketing can be tracked to provide the answer to whether or not the activity was a success or a failure. Don't be fooled by those who say that program results cannot be accurately tracked—failing to track your results will cost you money you can't afford to spend!

Change It Up

Nothing stays the same in business, and the marketing program is no exception. Based on the results, programs need to be deleted or modified and new programs added.

Landmine #16: *A marketing program should evolve with the company.*

Let's look again to *Tony's Fine Italian* restaurant to see how this might work.

> *Bruno and Tony consider what marketing mix to use to advertise the opening of their restaurant. Being new to the neighborhood, they decide to utilize the local newspaper to announce their grand opening. In addition, they decide to offer a free appetizer to anyone who comes in during their first week. Although Tony wants to fill the advertisement with stories of his grandmother and why her old-world recipes make their food better than anyone else's, Bruno convinces Tony that too much information will overwhelm the reader. They decide on a simple ad with the name of the restaurant, the location, and the free appetizer offer.*

New Business Landmines

They will also make individual prints of the ad to put on the bulletin boards at other local business establishments that are eager to help another new business in the neighborhood.

After a successful opening week and first month, Bruno and Tony begin to think about how to alter their marketing mix to maintain the momentum they built through their grand opening. They know it is important to keep their name "in the news" early on to build awareness. They decide to sponsor the local little league team and host a discount night for the entire league. Bruno and Tony know that through connecting with local groups and offering to support local activities, they can gain goodwill in the neighborhood and visits from their target customers.

Several months of success have now led Bruno and Tony to the next level of advertising. They have driven a lot of trial visits and are now trying to expand their customer base to include people who frequent other Italian restaurants in the area. To do this, they decide to alter their advertising to focus more on what differentiates their food from other restaurants'. They decide that the best way to do this is through a print ad in the community's Suburban Home magazine. Since the magazine is done every month, it will be viewed over a period of time and provide a great avenue to talk about how Tony's Fine Italian is based on Grandma's old-world recipes and how the restaurant uses local ingredients. Soon, people are coming in, eager to taste Tony's grandmother's rigatoni recipe!

As you can see, *Tony's Fine Italian* moved from trial and couponing to sponsorship to lifestyle-related print advertising within just a few short months. It is imperative that the business keep on top of its <u>marketing mix</u> to ensure relevance with both customers and the business.

Summary

Your marketing program starts with a clear and concise message, something your customers can easily understand. Once the marketing message is developed, a decision must be made whether to *optimize* or not. This decision is really a function of whether the business will get customers from the Internet or from other sources. Once the message and website are established, the owner/manager can consider the menu of other advertising and promotion options to develop the business's marketing mix. Whatever options you select, make sure to determine when and how to evaluate the success of each component of the program. If something is not working, try retooling the message or delivery and consider moving on to the next option.

8

SET THE PRICE HIGH, SO I MAKE MONEY!

In the book and movie *Jobs,* John Sculley (then Apple CEO) and the board wanted to price the Macintosh computer at $2,495 when it was launched. Steve Jobs, the company founder and creative force, was utterly against this, as his price target was $1,995. Sculley and the board simply looked at the cost to produce the Mac and felt that they couldn't make money at Jobs's price. Jobs's argument was based on what he felt the market would pay for the machine. In an intense boardroom scene in the movie, Jobs calls Sculley a "court jester" for his decision to price the Mac too high, which Jobs believed caused the product launch to fail.

As evidenced by the Macintosh story, pricing decisions can be difficult. There is no one formula to correctly price your product, but ultimately market-based pricing is what is needed. By market-based pricing, I mean that you must price the product or service at a level that customers will buy it. It doesn't have to be priced so low that every prospect will buy it, but it must be priced at a level that the business can generate enough sales to actually be in business.

Ultimately, the selling price must cover and exceed the cost to produce, but sometimes a product can start out with a lower price and increase over time. Other times, the opposite is true: a product is priced high to start, and then the price is reduced as sales and production increase and the unit cost to produce can be lowered through economies of scale (e.g., HDTVs and cell phones).

Again, there is no one pricing formula that I can provide to every new businessperson. There are, however, some general rules and considerations that are of value for almost any enterprise.

Cost Plus Pricing

Generally, all would probably agree that, in concept, the price of a product or service should be based on its value to the customer and the price of competitive products or services—again, what I refer to as market-based pricing. However, that's usually where the agreement ends—at the conceptual level.

> **Landmine #17:** *There is no guarantee that you can sell your product or service for more than it costs!*

I cannot tell you how many businesspeople feel that they are entitled to a profit. Hence, they feel they can price their product or service *cost plus* (i.e., pricing the product or service at its actual cost, plus a certain percentage added on to the costs). Many businesspeople use cost plus regardless of whether it will push the selling price well above where competitive products are priced.

I was working in partnership with an architect who had brought his son and son-in-law into the business and had expanded his services to include construction management for single-family houses.

The partnership was straightforward; I would buy the land (and put up the money to do so) and secure financing for the construction. The architect would design the house, and his boys would supervise the construction. I would then market and sell the house (through realtors), and any profits would be split fifty-fifty.

Things started fine. (There was a market back then, so yes, we could actually sell houses.) We were doing reasonably well, not making much money, but we were a start-up, so I was satisfied with the results.

I could tell, however, that the architect was not happy, so I called a meeting. In short, the architect felt that I was selling the houses at too low of a price, which of course was limiting his 50-percent share of the profits. To address his concern, I reviewed each house sale with him in detail and discussed the marketing and sales strategy, the competition, and the various offers received. In short, I justified the selling price for each house, one by one, based on all of these factors.

Unfortunately, I could see that the architect wasn't buying it. When I finished, the architect said, "Gary, you don't understand what I am saying." The architect then went on to describe in detail his sons' personal financial situation and how much money each of them needed to make. He then related their "target" salaries to our current sales volume to arrive at what he needed to make on each house to cover their living expenses. Cost plus! What he was saying was, "I want to pay my boys this, so we need to price our houses at a level high enough to cover their pay"—his cost—regardless of what the market is or how other houses nearby were priced.

I, of course, tried to explain that the selling prices for the houses would have to be a function of the market, not what we wanted to make on each house. I pointed out that the real analysis was how many houses the boys would need to build annually in order to generate enough profit to fund their salaries, but this point never even registered. In other words, I tried to tell him that the boys would have to work much harder to really earn what he wanted to pay them.

The partnership ended fairly soon thereafter. I noticed that several houses that the architect and his sons had built were sitting for extended periods of time unsold. I wonder why? Hmmm.

So if cost plus is not the best pricing mechanism, how should the business determine market-based pricing? The answer depends partly on what is being sold and how. The business concept and marketing message are also integrally related to pricing.

Competing Based on Price

If the main product selling point (i.e., marketing message) is that the business has the lowest prices, pricing is relatively easy. Your business's prices need to be lower than the competition's. In practical terms, if the focus is to deliver a lower price, prices need to be low enough to attract customers to the product or service and away from the competition's. Determining what that price is may take some time and even some trial and error.

My suggestion is to price at the low end of the price range to start, so that prices do not have to be reduced later. This approach doesn't work well for a high-end custom home builder who only sells eight houses a year. However, it works fine for many products and services. No one ever likes to see the price of something that they just purchased go down; it tends to leave a bad taste in people's mouths.

A note of caution: do not price too low, or people may believe that your product or service is inferior to the competition's. This gets to the fact that people don't trust anyone anymore. If your product is priced too low, people may feel that it must be inferior in terms of quality.

There are multiple ways to deliver a lower price than the competition. One way is to simply price all of the products lower. Alternatively, the business can price certain products lower and advertise those "deals" to attract customers to the product line.

Low prices can also be offered through discounts—coupons, vouchers, certificates, or other promotions. This allows a business to maintain higher list prices but to market the lower discounted prices. JC Penney recently embarked on a catastrophic pricing strategy of "everyday low prices" versus their older, somewhat tried-and-true practice of periodic advertising of sales and discounts.

The everyday low prices didn't work. It can and does work for some, like a Walmart, but it certainly didn't work for JC Penney. Penney's customers had been trained to buy when the big sales were advertised. No big sale—no reason to go to Penney's.

Depending on how large your business is relative to the competition, it is important to monitor how competitors react to your pricing. Don't expect your competitors to sit idly by while your company steals their customers by charging 3 percent less than they are. Many competitors will fight back—compete! They may match your lower prices or offer other incentives to their customers that your business cannot easily match. Be ready and attuned to the market; know what your competition is doing. Competing on price can be very effective, but it can also get nasty.

Free-Form Pricing

In the end, the product or service must be priced to sell. Of course, the business must make money, but there are many ways to get to a profit if there are sales (e.g., cut administrative costs, increase employee productivity). If the product or service isn't selling, it is impossible to make a profit.

> **Landmine #18:** *Pricing is more art than science. If possible, start at the lower end of the range. Monitor the impact of price changes closely.*

How did Steve Jobs know that the market would pay $1,995 for a Mac but not pay $2,495? *It's* hard to say—maybe Jobs wasn't right either; maybe the initial Mac would not have sold at any price, or maybe it would have sold at $995 but not $1,995. The point is that the key is to focus on more than production cost when pricing the product or service. The *owner/manager* must take into account many factors when making the pricing decisions, including competitors' prices, the ultimate value of the product or service to the customer, initial versus longer-term pricing options, production costs and how they may change over time, and the relationship between the marketing message and pricing.

I have seen most new businesses price either using "cost plus" or their competitors' prices. So if new business owners feel that their product or service is better than the competition's, they may price slightly higher. In the end, the market will tell you whether your pricing is optimal.

Closely monitor how different prices change your sales. It is important to try to isolate the impact of specific business decisions and actions as much as possible. Sales were up this week or month? Great, but try to find out why. Were sales up because of a Groupon offer or a newspaper ad run last week? Were other types of price discounts offered last week? Were the salespeople different? Was their pitch different? Or were more people just in town because summer is over and people are back from their vacations and summer homes?

The answers to these questions are critical to managing the business and establishing the most effective pricing and sales strategy. This is difficult, and even experienced managers can disagree on the facts and how to interpret them.

One of my businesses had a sales center at a resort in Palm Springs selling time-shares and travel products to guests at the resort. The salespeople gave a one-and-a-half-hour sales presentation to guests, who were given a gift to listen. Selling prices ranged from as low as $2,000 up to $5,000. There were three salespeople. The salespeople were given a minimum price for each product but were allowed to sell at a higher price and get a higher commission. Therefore, selling prices ranged from as low as $2,000 up to $5,000.

After three months of sales, I began to see a pattern. One salesperson, Fred, who generally set prices higher, was selling much less than his peers. Said another way, his closing percentage was lower, at approximately 10 percent (he sold at one out of ten presentations). On the other extreme, Randi, who was very aggressive in dropping prices, was closing over 30 percent of her prospects. Xavier was in the middle.

I discussed with my partners the above observations and suggested that prices needed to be lowered to maximize volume and sales. My partners were dead set against this strategy. They felt that the company should be pushing prices even higher! Their belief was that the salespeople were not selling "hard enough" and that the higher prices were attainable if the salespeople just did a better job.

Somewhat astonished by their position, I decided to do a detailed, written analysis (shown below) in which I charted each salesperson's closing percentage and average selling price for each of the prior three months. The graph below shows the average selling prices on the bottom, horizontal axis, and the closing percentage on the left-side, vertical axis. After the graph was done, I drew the curve showing the relationship between the average selling price and the closing percentage.

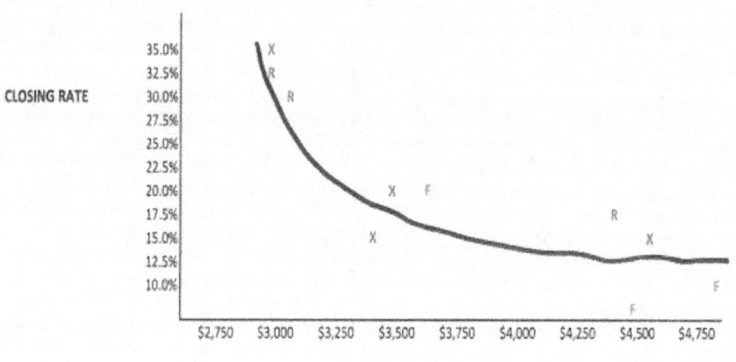

X - Monthly average price and closing rates for Xavier
R - Monthly average price and closing rates for Randi
F - Monthly average price and closing rates for Fred

I felt that this chart confirmed my suspicions that the lower selling prices were generating significantly higher sales volume and profits. At a price of approximately $3,000, the company was selling to almost one-third of the prospects, but when the selling price was pushed up to $4,500, the company was only selling to one out of eight! Even for the one month when Fred (the poorest salesperson) dropped his average selling price to approximately $3,600, he improved his closing percentage to 20 percent (one in five prospects sold); and when Randi (the best salesperson) moved her price up into the $4,500 price range one month, her closing percentage dropped below 20 percent!

I felt that this was a pretty compelling analysis. I believed that it would lead to my partners finally agreeing that lower prices would improve the bottom line. However, my partners still would not agree and again blocked my attempts to reduce selling prices across the board.

Needless to say, sales floundered after that date for several months. Ultimately, we added additional product enhancements and raised prices even more. The business closed six months later.

This story demonstrates how difficult pricing decisions can be, and that there is tremendous subjectivity that comes into play.

The Sales Process

Some services and products require limited or no selling. All that is required is creating awareness through marketing programs. Others require significant explanation and selling effort.

For example, a hair salon doesn't need to exert much effort to sell. Generally when customers come in the door, possibly in response to an advertisement, they have already decided that they need the service—a haircut, color, or style—and they probably have a pretty good idea of approximately what they should pay. So the selling effort is typically as simple as a receptionist or stylist greeting the customers and asking them what service they are seeking.

On the other hand, a car requires significant selling. The marketing may be similar to what the hair salon uses, a newspaper advertisement, but the similarities end there.

I don't know the exact statistics, but I am sure that a very high percentage of prospects walking into a hair salon actually buy something. However, the number of people walking into a car dealership who buy would be much smaller. The difference is not only due to the much higher cost of a car, but also because the person walking into the car dealership has to be sold on the product. The person walking into the hair salon is really already sold. He or she can only be put off by abnormally high prices, being ignored by the staff, or an unsavory environment.

Direct Sales

Depending on the product or service, the business may need to employ salespeople, as a car dealership does.

> **Landmine #19:** *Salespeople are driven by cash, really not much else. Keep their commission structure simple, calculate commissions on gross sales, and pay early and on time to recruit and retain the best.*

Salespeople are always overpaid; that's just the way it works, so get used to it. In some companies, the top salespeople can actually make more than the CEO and CFO. Salespeople need to be compensated according to industry standards and local market conditions. Certainly, your businesses can treat salespeople better than the competition does, and that can help you recruit better quality people, but in the end, the best salespeople are driven by dollars—their commissions.

Recently my right-hand financial person, Craig, became extremely frustrated dealing with the salespeople in one of my businesses.

Even though we had spent endless hours working with and training the salespeople, they continued to make errors in completing the sales agreements with customers and continued to sell outside of the parameters that we had established.

After letting Craig vent about his ongoing frustrations in dealing with our rogue salespeople and his inability to understand how they could not follow the simple set of rules that we had laid out, I simply told him the following: "It is hopeless. They will never completely change. They are whores who only think about making their commission. Don't even try to understand them; they are on a different planet from you. You will never be able to understand or truly control all of their actions. You just need to monitor, redirect where you can, and try to keep them pointed in the right direction."

A good salesperson will do almost anything to get the deal done. This is good, but it obviously creates risk for you—the risk of misrepresentation and, ultimately, of lawsuits. Therefore, manage your sales force closely; know what your salespeople are doing and what they are saying. Documentation needs to be standardized and reviewed to ensure that it is properly completely. Salespeople need to know that the sales documents are being reviewed. To be clear, don't stifle sales creativity, but make sure that the salespeople know that even though you support them and their efforts, you are monitoring them.

As stated above, commissions should be easy to understand and calculate. A percentage of gross sales is always preferable. Complex commission schedules are a deterrent to sales because they get salespeople confused, which is never good.

Summary

Sales and pricing decisions are dependent upon the business. There is as much art as there is science in pricing decisions. Use market-based pricing, not cost plus. Monitor changes closely to see what impact they may have on your sales.

9

I'll Do the Accounting in My Spare Time

Many athletes start charities to give back to the community, which is obviously nice. However, the results are often not great. A recent article in the *Chicago Tribune* stated, "The *Tribune's* analysis of 79 charities and foundations started by athletes who have played here in the last decade found nearly half of the organizations were dissolved." The *Tribune's* comment on one specific charity is telling: "the former Bears defensive tackle learned it [his charity] had lost track of a large sum of money."[1] Lost track? Really? Unfortunately, this is not unusual. Often these well-intentioned attempts to help others are not set up with professional accountants and money managers who have the necessary experience and integrity to properly keep track of things. Instead, friends or social worker types are often put in charge of the accounting and cash management with the results already mentioned above.

Stupid athletes, right? Hardly. I can't tell you how many new businesspeople do the exact same thing. They either have no

---

[1] Jared S. Hopkins, "Pros Are Often Amateurs Running Charities," *Chicago Tribune*, December 22, 2013, sec. 3.

accounting and financial support or have their spouse or brother-in-law helping part-time because he or she was a bookkeeper twenty years ago or took an accounting course in college.

Every business needs to provide adequate resources to ensure that this "back-office" work is done and done properly.

What is the work? Billings and collections, approving and processing invoices (i.e., bills), depositing cash and reconciling bank accounts, processing payroll and payroll taxes, budgeting cash, and forecasting and preparing monthly accounting statements and year-end tax returns. All this work, plus more, must be done and done regularly, not after the end of the year.

So you need to devote resources to making sure this work gets done. However, there is a balance that needs to be reached. It is certainly possible to invest too much time and money in completing these tasks.

Accounting for Accountants

Only build accounting and back-office systems that are needed to manage the business effectively, not to keep your accountant happy.

> **Landmine #20:** *Don't let your financial people build an overly detailed accounting system. Build a system that allows the business to file its taxes and, more importantly, to provide owners/managers the information that they need to make decisions and manage cash.*

Many businesses end up creating accounting systems that provide too much detail—too many line items (i.e., accounts), for example. The litmus test is: What information does management need to evaluate the business? Does management of a restaurant really need to have its accounting people break out purchases of ketchup versus mustard? Probably not. On the other hand, management would certainly want to keep track of beverage versus food costs. Given that many accountants love detail, it is incumbent upon the business _owners/managers_ to monitor their accountants and direct them only to produce the level of detail really needed.

Internal Controls

No _owners/managers_ want their employees to steal from them. However, the prudent owner/manager must weigh the cost of preventing a theft against the cost of the theft itself. For example, most businesses, not all, assume that the cost of preventing the theft of small amounts of office supplies by their staff is not worth the cost and headaches associated with keeping Post-its under lock and key.

An additional consideration is the impact on morale if employees are treated like criminals. Employees may rightfully feel that if they can't be trusted with the Post-its, they are not really valued and important members of the organization. So in my opinion, an owner/manager shouldn't sweat the small stuff.

I am not suggesting that a restaurant owner/manager watch his or her employees load up bags with wine and beer every night before they go home. Quite the contrary: I believe that employees who are caught stealing should be terminated. My philosophy is that employees need to be treated with respect and trust until they do something that clearly demonstrates that they are not worthy of such treatment. Once employees prove that they are no longer worthy of respect and trust, they should be immediately terminated.

I am also not suggesting that a business have no internal controls. Cash and inventory must be monitored closely and discrepancies investigated immediately. A detailed review of monthly financial statement variances can also help point out theft or misappropriation of funds. For example, if beverage cost at a restaurant has been running 30 percent of sales for twelve months and the cost increases to 35 percent, it's probably time to investigate the difference and monitor bar activity more closely.

Options for Back-Office Help

Depending on the size and complexity of your business, consider outsourcing some or all of these functions. There are Internet payroll companies that will inexpensively process the payroll, including calculating taxes, filing tax returns, and making tax payments. There are also many local accounting firms that will handle your bookkeeping and other back-office functions.

If you choose to try to handle this work internally or with the help of a family member to save a few bucks, the test of whether this is okay is whether: (1) all bank accounts are reconciled monthly and *differences investigated and resolved,* and (2) all bills are getting prepared and mailed to customers/clients on a timely basis and past-due accounts are getting phone calls to collect past-due balances. As long as these two tasks are getting completed on a timely basis, it's okay to continue handling them internally; otherwise, it's time to get help.

Summary

Every business needs to provide for basic accounting and administrative tasks. The accounting system should be designed to provide management with the information it needs to support decision making and managing cash. Excess details are costly and unnecessary.

10

Government Won't Bother Me—I'm a Little Guy!

The asshole politicians in Washington, DC, and the state capitals constantly sing the praises of small business, while they continually kick us in the teeth. This is a fact. Honestly, the existing regulations are more than any small business can possibly comply with, which of course leaves <u>owner/managers</u> exposed to bureaucratic penalties and lawsuits. In fact, anyone who really fully understood the regulatory and tax environment would rightfully ask, "How and why would I even try to start a new business?" Thankfully, most entrepreneurs do not fully appreciate the regulatory, legal, and tax burdens that they are embracing when they start, so new businesses start all the time.

So what is a prudent entrepreneur to do? If compliance with all of the requirements is not possible, should they all be ignored? Or must every new business have a full-time attorney on staff to keep track of all of the regulations and ensure compliance? The answer lies somewhere in between.

Government Won't Bother Me—I'm a Little Guy!

Landmine #21: *It is impossible to comply with all government regulations, but it is stupid not to comply with any.*

Certainly, identify and comply with the easy and more significant regulations—basic business licensing, legal entity formation and registration, IRS filings, written employee policies, and the posting of employee notices. Additional compliance depends on the nature of the business.

> *I have a cousin who is a small-scale organic vegetable farmer who sells directly to restaurants and at farmers' markets. This cousin was blown away by the overarching requirements for a "processing facility" technically required if he "packaged" his products for sale. However, the definition of "packaging" did not seem to include simply putting his organic vegetables in a brown paper bag. This loophole of sorts seems to allow my cousin to skip the $10,000 investment in building a "processing facility," which is really nothing more than a certain kind of countertop and sink with a foot pedal to operate the faucet (very expensive) located in a separate room built with specific materials and lighting. Personally, I think that my cousin was right not to invest this $10,000 to comply with the technical "letter of the law."*

The good news is that the politicians have now passed so many laws that enforcement is impossible. The bad news is that this exposes all of us to piecemeal and inconsistent enforcement. Sometimes new bureaucrats get hired and are enthusiastic about their new jobs, so they start enforcing regulations that have been ignored for years by the older, retiring bureaucrats. This happens all of the time, and every business owner is subject to this kind of harassment.

How do you identify what regulations are related to your business? Some people are afraid to, and they prefer to stick their heads in the sand. I can't support this approach, so my advice is to ask. I am not a big fan of surprises, so I would rather know up front what the bureaucrats want from my business.

Call your state employment office on a "no-name" basis and ask what notices should be published for employees. Go to the local municipal business licensing office and tell the staff generally what kind of business you want to start and ask about licensing requirements. Call your local building department official and ask what permits are needed to renovate your space and what they cost.

Attorneys can also be helpful. As part of setting up your new business entity, licensing and other requirements should also be addressed. However, as discussed further in chapter 11, please remember that corporate attorneys are not experts in human resources, so they will not necessarily advise you of all of the requirements in every area.

Employees versus Independent Contractors

Employees cost you "lotsa" money, a real "lotsa" money! Therefore, every business needs to evaluate whether any or all of the people that it needs to operate the business can be independent contractors (I/Cs) or whether they must be employees. This decision can save the business money, but it also exposes the company to challenge.

The taxing authorities are not real fond of the use of I/Cs for obvious reasons—the business is not paying any payroll taxes, unemployment taxes, and workers' comp insurance and there are no tax withholdings. Instead, the business issues every independent contractor a 1099-MISC tax form after year-end, listing the amount paid to the I/C during the prior tax year. The I/C is then responsible for paying taxes, including self-employment taxes (i.e., Social Security and Medicare taxes). In reality, many I/Cs do not file tax forms properly or fully claim all of the amounts paid to them, so again, the taxing folks really frown on I/Cs.

To be clear, I am not suggesting that your business turn employees into I/Cs. There are fairly extensive rules on what constitutes an I/C versus an employee. Instead, I am suggesting that you review these rules (available online) and possibly consult with a tax accountant to determine whether any of the staff for the business can be properly classified as I/Cs. I also have several YouTube videos that I have done discussing the differences between ICs and employees. These are available online, and you should be able to find them by simply Googling my name.

Assuming that the business can use I/Cs, it goes without saying that they need to be treated as I/Cs and not as employees. Surprisingly, this basic truth is routinely ignored over and over again by many small business people. Ignoring this rule exposes the business to reclassification of the I/Cs as employees, which can lead to back payroll taxes, interest, penalties, and maybe more trouble.

An example e-mail that I sent to one of my clients who had a history of struggling with the terminology differences between I/Cs and employees follows:

Here are the issues for this person who we were told in the attached e-mail would be a 1099 independent contractor:
1. *The person received an "offer letter," which is typically what employees get. I/Cs sign a contract.*
2. *The offer letter says: "this is a salaried position." Again, this strongly implies employee. I/Cs don't get a position and don't get a salary. They agree to perform a service and get paid a fee for doing so. The fee gets paid pursuant to the contract terms and invoices that the I/C sends the company.*

3. The company doesn't typically pay workers' comp on I/Cs, so in addition to adding to the employee vs. I/C problems, the statement is just false, as the person is not covered by your workers' comp.
4. I also doubt that your general liability policy fully covers an I/C. So again, telling the person that he or she is covered implies that he or she is in fact an employee.
5. The "team" references in your letter are also not great but are the least problematic. Usually an I/C is just that—independent—so not really part of the "team."
6. You had the person complete a W-4 and I-9. These forms are for employees. I/Cs complete a W-9, not these two forms.

Again, at this point you likely have no argument to pay this person as an I/C. As such, if you proceed on that basis, the company is exposed to paying 15.3 percent in FICA and Medicare taxes, plus interest and penalties.

If you want to continue to treat these people as I/Cs, you should destroy all of the old documentation and ask each person to do the same. You should instead come up with an I/C agreement (I can supply a sample I/C Agreement) and have one signed by each person. The people should send you invoices on their invoice forms once or twice per month.

Doing the above will not provide a fail-safe position that these people are I/Cs; however, it will at least put you in a position to make the argument. Ultimately, the determination of I/C vs. employee status is based on an assessment of each position. The IRS guidelines that I sent in my earlier e-mail (attached again to this e-mail) are the best way to make this determination.

Per my earlier e-mail, getting "caught" on the I/C vs. employee issue is significantly more likely than getting caught on income tax issues. There are many ways companies get "caught." By way of example, a disgruntled contractor goes to collect unemployment insurance and gets told that he or she has none. Then this individual takes his or her *"offer letter"* down to the local DOL office and says that the company screwed him or her. The DOL is also conducting regular audits, much more often than the IRS.

To start, don't call I/Cs employees. Don't give them an employee policy manual; instead have them sign an I/C agreement that has policies and procedures for I/Cs. Don't advertise for them using words like *employees* or *associates*. Don't set definitive hours for them. Don't give them medical or other benefits. Remember, in concept, an I/C works for himself or herself, and is providing services to the business as a consultant or third-party contractor. Treat your I/Cs as such.

One last point about I/Cs is that many have become rather savvy. If they feel that your business has wronged them, they are not afraid to go to the local department of labor office and describe in detail how your business is hiring employees but forcing them to be I/Cs to cheat them out of benefits and cheat the government out of taxes.

Taxes

You must declare your income, period. Even if it is cash, you must declare it. People get in real trouble for not declaring income because there is really no defense. "Oh really, Mr. IRS man, cash sales are still sales?" Hopefully, the fallacy of this statement is obvious. On the other hand, deductions are a whole different situation. There is almost always some support or explanation that can be offered to support a deduction. In short, declare your income, and work hard to maximize your deductions.

Landmine #22: *Don't fall into a trap. Declare your income (even cash sales!) for taxes, and then be aggressive on tax deductions.*

Most state governments require that sales taxes be paid. Whether they need to be paid monthly or quarterly depends typically on volume. Again, pay the sales taxes.

The nuances and tradeoffs of corporate taxes versus "flow-through" tax entities are discussed in chapter 4 on organization, so I will not repeat the discussion here.

Summary

Only a fool fails to secure basic business licenses and other operating permits for his or her business. Ask the bureaucrats (on a no-name basis) or your attorney what licenses and permits are needed to operate. It is important to look at independent contractor versus employee status for staffing needs. If you have work that can be done by independent contractors, make sure that they are not treated like employees. Dot the *i*'s and cross the *t*'s on this one! Play no games with cash sales; declare them for tax purposes. Save your money by being aggressive on deductions.

11

Devil's Triangle: Lawyers, Lawsuits & Litigation

Attorneys are a part of business life and must be employed when appropriate. With that said, heed the next landmine!

Landmine #23: *If you do everything your attorney tells you, you will probably fail.*

First point: a good attorney knows the law in his or her area of expertise, not necessarily in other areas. So going to an attorney who specializes in patent law for advice on a real estate transaction is like going to a dentist for hip-replacement surgery. Attorneys specialize, even though it is not as readily apparent as it is for doctors, so go to an attorney who works in the area where you need help.

Second, good attorneys know the law. They are not financial consultants, accountants, marriage counselors, or management consultants, and from my experience, most are not even good negotiators. (I think the reason is because the law is about right and wrong, while negotiations are about reaching solutions that work, regardless of who is right or wrong.)

Second Opinions

An attorney is a tool, a required tool in today's world, but a tool. Attorneys are to be managed and used, and their opinions are to be considered. However, their opinions must be challenged and tested, sometimes with a second opinion. It's interesting that most people don't hesitate to get a second opinion on a medical issue, but would never even consider going to a second attorney for another opinion.

Even successful businessmen and smart people rely too heavily on attorneys and don't seek to challenge or test their opinions. There are many times when an attorney will give his or her client no acceptable alternatives. In these cases, the <u>*owner/managers*</u> must challenge their counsel to explain the "downside risk" from not taking their legal advice and to assess the likelihood that the downside will occur. Businesspeople are often confronted with two imperfect alternatives and have to select the one they believe to be best. The situation is the same with legal issues. Sometimes there is no perfect answer, so the owner/manager must get all the facts and assess the risks from making a less-than-perfect choice. The point is to never be afraid to say to your attorney, "What could happen if I don't take your advice?" The answer to this question can often be very enlightening.

Sue the Bastards!

Lawsuits are to be avoided—how's that for some quality advice? For those who think that justice can be obtained through the courts, you are flat wrong. It is certainly possible to run up huge legal bills by litigating, but you very rarely can get justice through the court system on civil matters.

Landmine #24: *Lawsuits make attorneys rich, not the litigants.*

Suing out of anger is a really, really bad idea. For times when litigation is the only avenue available, you must develop a plan or strategy up front: What are the goals of the litigation? What would an adequate settlement/outcome look like? How much money will it cost to litigate the claim? Only with this knowledge can you make a prudent decision whether to sue or not.

Can You Collect on a Judgment?

Remember, even with a judgment from a court in your favor, there is still the matter of collecting the amount awarded. Most people don't realize this fact. Yes, companies and people routinely ignore a court's order and continue not to pay.

For example, one of my companies that had been successful, but after a number of years failed due to the impact of the Great Recession, owned a restaurant that was shut down. The cash that was available after the shutdown along with the outstanding bills were totaled. I sent letters to all creditors (e.g., suppliers and vendors) explaining the situation and offering a settlement amount. In short, I offered to pay out all of the remaining cash to the creditors. Unfortunately, the remaining cash was considerably less than what the creditors were owed. The alternative was to declare bankruptcy, in which case the attorneys would have gotten all of the remaining cash, and the suppliers and vendors nothing.

Some vendors took the settlement and received a check, and others did not.

One of the vendors who did not accept the settlement later decided to pursue the matter through the court system. We sent the vendor a letter and explained that the cash was now gone, as it had been paid out to the vendors willing to settle, and that he should not waste any more time or money taking us to court, as there was no money left in the company to pay his claim. The vendor ignored our response and took us to small claims court anyway. We didn't show up, so the vendor got a judgment against the company in the amount of his unpaid bills and probably some interest.

The vendor then triumphantly sent us the judgment and again insisted on now being paid. We sent another letter back to the vendor explaining that we were sorry that he had wasted more time and money going to court, but the judgment had really changed nothing. Our company still had no cash or other assets to pay him, with or without a judgment, so there would be no payment forthcoming.

It seems that the vendor finally figured it out because that was the last we heard from him.

Justice in the courts; sorry, none is available.

Now What—I Am a Defendant?

Almost any company that stays in business long enough will get sued, and possibly the owner/mangers themselves will too. There are many reasons why, but suffice it to say that we live in a litigious society. Although I haven't done an analysis, my belief is that the employees are the most likely of any group to sue, then the owner/managers (suing each other), followed by trade vendors/suppliers, and finally the customers (assuming that you plan to operate a legitimate business).

Is It Ripe Yet?

When sued, the business must fight legal claims until they are "*ripe*" and then move aggressively to settle.

> **Landmine #25:** *Fighting lawsuits endlessly is a waste of time and money. Find the right time—usually after you throw a few punches—and then settle them.*

Regardless of the lawsuit or threatened claim, there is a concept that I call "ripeness." No, I am not discussing a fruit stand; I am still talking about legal claims. As much as I hate litigation, as a defendant you cannot rush or push through settlements of claims too quickly. Offering a settlement too early is usually seen by the other side as a sign of weakness, which will just embolden the person suing you. Instead, you must *fight fiercely* until the claim or suit is "ripe," at which point it can be settled.

Why? A couple reasons to consider. First, the people on the other side are probably mad, so they need time to cool down and enjoy the wonderful experience of paying their attorneys to litigate. In short, after two or three legal bills from their counsel, their anger will start shifting from you to their attorneys. This, of course, means that the better and more prominent the other side's legal counsel (resulting in higher billing rates), the better position your company will be in to work a settlement.

Many managers feel better when the other side engages a small, unknown attorney. Not me. I want to see the person suing my company hire the best, most expensive counsel that he or she can get. This accelerates the "ripeness factor" of the case.

As noted above, before the claim is ripe, your business must fight and typically should not offer to settle. I can't give you a rule for determining when every case is ripe. I would suggest that typically right before discovery is a good time to consider whether the claim is "ripe." Once the plaintiffs get well into discovery, they may have invested too much in legal bills, making them feel obligated to proceed. It makes no sense, but it's the way people think.

The second reason not to settle before the case is "ripe" is that your business may get a reputation as an easy mark with plaintiff attorneys and other potential claimants. This is especially true for employee claims. It must seem painful and costly to get a settlement out of your business, or believe me, others will follow the path forged by other plaintiff attorneys.

Your attorney, unless he or she is really top-notch, will not know when to settle. This means that the _owner/manager_ must actively manage the claim. Sitting back and just letting your attorney handle litigation is a costly mistake.

Know Your Opponent

Even as a middle school football coach—tougher job than you might expect!—I scouted the other team. I wanted to know as much as possible about my opponents. Lawsuits are no different. It is critical to find out as much as possible about the attorney representing the people suing your company. Most likely, given the fraternity of lawyers (and politicians, for that matter), your attorney will know the opposing counsel or can at least find out information about him or her. This is important to know.

It is also important to evaluate who is really controlling the claim against you: the attorney or the client. Knowing who the decision maker really is on the other side is very important in the timing and amount of the settlement offer. Settlement offers have to be tailored to ensure that the decision maker is going to benefit. Obviously, your business can't offer to pay the opposing counsel, but the settlement offer can be structured in a way to appeal to the opposing counsel.

Let's assume that the opposing counsel is working on a contingency basis (instead of billing for his or her time, the attorney is going to take a percentage of the settlement or judgment, if any). Contingency attorneys typically do not want to spend _lotsa_ time on claims that they are not sure that they can win. Consequently, as soon as your attorney at least presents some facts to opposing counsel that might lead to questions about the strength of the other side's claim, the claim may be "ripe." The reason is because now that opposing counsel knows that there is some risk to his or her case, the attorney will be more willing to take an early settlement and get something without having to invest any more of his or her own time and effort.

Employee Lawsuits—Sexual Harassment

Employees can sue for a number of reasons, with harassment, wrongful termination, and broken compensation promises high on the list. Sexual harassment is becoming one of the most common employee legal claims. It is an easy claim these days. (Actually, all claims are easy; employees just need an attorney to file any trumped-up claim that they like.) From my personal experience I would say that this is especially true in the food service business, but such claims can arise from almost any business environment, and both men and women do not need to be present.

Landmine #26: *Ignore sexual harassment at your own risk.*

I believe that the reason there are so many sexual harassment claims is that the law makes behavior that would be acceptable at a party or friend's house unacceptable at work. As society becomes more and more open in the media and everyday life to sex, the US Congress has created special rules for conduct in the workplace that are more strict than everyplace else.

Obviously, I am not talking about unwarranted sexual advances; these are inappropriate anywhere. However, there is much conduct that qualifies as sexual harassment in the workplace that is not uncommon outside of work. For example, certain billboards have pictures of scantily clad women that would be considered grounds for harassment if posted in the workplace by one of your employees.

Furthermore, most companies and most successful business managers, in spite of extensive training programs and long, detailed written policies, do not know how to handle sexual harassment claims. In my opinion a very large percentage of such claims would never rise to the level of litigation if they were properly handled from the outset.

The reason sexual harassment claims are mishandled is because the claims typically first come to the attention of a middle manager. Managers are supposed to try to solve problems, right? So what the does the manager do? He or she will typically get the accuser and alleged perpetrator in his or her office and then try to work it out. Often with statements like: "You two are acting like children! What the hell is wrong with you? Don't you know that our business is struggling? We don't have time for this kind of bull. I need both of you to assure me that you can act like adults and work together, okay? Okay, now get back to work!"

This is not exactly what the accuser is looking for, especially if the claim is valid. Whether valid or not, the manager has now unknowingly enflamed the situation and exposed your business to a lawsuit. Why? Because the situation has not been resolved, even though the manager thinks it has been.

When a claim of sexual harassment is made, it must be taken seriously. Taking it seriously means: (1) separating the accused and accuser to prevent any chance of further harassment—this means no communication between the parties, (2) investigating the claims, and (3) based on the evidence, resolving the matter in accordance with the company's written policy regarding harassment.

Unfortunately, in cases of sexual harassment, <u>owner/managers</u> can neither assume innocence or guilt. Instead, once a claim is made, until it is investigated, the owner/managers must try to neutralize the situation until they can figure out what has happened. As stated above, separate the accuser and accused, and insist, under penalty of termination, that there be no communication between them—*none!*

Yes, that means there cannot even be an apology! *No* communication at all. If the accuser tries to make it better, believe me, it will only get worse—a lot worse—for the business. Think about it. If the accused apologizes, even if he or she did nothing wrong, the accuser (and his or her attorney) now has some pretty strong evidence that your workplace does in fact harbor sexual harassment.

At Tony's Fine Italian, Tony hires two waiters, Mary and John. After six weeks' employment, Mary accuses John of sexual harassment. She makes the accusations to Tony in writing. When John learns of Mary's claim, before Tony can get to him, he corners Mary and sincerely apologizes.

John and Mary may now be reconciled to each other, but John has given Mary a "smoking gun"—the apology—to come after Tony and Bruno's business for a large claim! Can't you hear the plaintiff's attorney now? "Well, of course, Mr. Judge, Mary's claims are valid. John even apologized to Mary for his behavior. Why would John apologize if he did nothing wrong?"

John, embarrassed by the whole incident, ends up quitting and moves on with his life, and Bruno and Tony are stuck paying for his inconsiderate and poor behavior.

Bruno and Tony discussed the entire incident with their HR consultant, who told them what they should have done:

- *Send John home immediately with pay. Tell him he is on "administrative leave" with full pay and benefits, while the company investigates the claim.*
- *John cannot be treated as guilty, fired, or sent home without pay, and he cannot be treated as innocent until proven guilty.*
- *Allow Mary to continue to work but give her the opportunity to take some time off with pay to recover from the trauma.*
- *Have an HR consultant interview John, Mary, and other staff to investigate the claim.*

- *If it looks like John is guilty, adhere to the company's written policy and terminate John if it is a second offense or suspend him without pay for a month for a first offense, depending on the severity of the harassment.*
- *If it looks like John is innocent, bring John back to work, but still have him meet with the HR consultant to discuss sexual harassment further. Offer Mary counseling and have her meet with the HR consultant to further explain what sexual harassment is and is not. Do not fire Mary, even if her claims are suspicious.*

The bottom line is that as soon as a claim comes up, it is going to cost the business money, either in settlement and legal fees or in training and lost employee and management time. Regardless, the business loses.

So how can a business prevent a claim? Serious training can help. Putting all employees in a room and having them watch a thirty-minute video isn't really very serious. Hiring better quality people can help, but we have even had a president (of the United States) who made sexual advances to an employee, so I'm not sure about that one. It is probably best that the policy be written, posted, and clear and that it be discussed among employee groups. Employees need to know that management cares and is serious about enforcing harassment policies. Some examples of things owner/managers must do:

- The motorcycle calendar with the girls in bikinis is just inappropriate for work, so make your dishwasher take it down.
- The chef who loves to tell dirty jokes needs to be told to stop.
- The waiter who likes to give neck and shoulder massages needs to be instructed that this isn't happening in your restaurant.

This makes you a killjoy, right? Well write your senator, but in the meantime, to prevent claims, these are the types of actions it will take!

Finally, and a lot of people disagree with me on this one, create a "hot line": an 800 number (costs ten dollars a month) and an e-mail address that goes directly to your HR person and the <u>owner/ managers</u>, where anyone can report a possible instance of sexual harassment. I personally think this can help nip things in the bud before they expand into a full-blown sexual harassment–type issue. Usually when harassment claims come forward, it's not because of one joke or one instance; it is usually because of an ongoing pattern that is never dealt with.

Assuming that the company's policy is that any possible claim must be reported and there is an e-mail and 800 number in place, making reporting claims easy, an accuser who waits until he or she has been harassed for ten weeks has given your attorney a pretty good argument that the accuser did not comply with company policy and hence prevented the company from preventing the harassment. In other words, the accuser is responsible because he or she didn't report it. Not a great argument, but it's something.

<u>Legal Agreements</u>

Do you have to hire an attorney to draft every legal document that you will use in your business? Not necessarily, but it ultimately depends on your own level of experience and the types of legal documents that you need. It is true that many different types of documents are available from various online services today at relatively low prices. Can you use these documents to meet some of your business's needs? Of course, but I would still suggest that any key documents be at least reviewed by outside legal counsel. There are many nuances in the law in each state, and sometimes something as simple as not capitalizing certain words can negate their impact and effect.

Summary

I could go on for endless pages on lawsuits, but I think that I have covered enough for the new entrepreneur. The business must have an employee policy manual that clearly covers sexual harassment. If your business gets sued, get a good attorney, but manage the attorney and look for a "ripe" spot to settle. Never sue in anger, unless money means nothing. Never expect to receive justice through the legal system; it's better to rely on your own negotiating skills to settle a claim.

12

JUST BUY A BUSINESS

Sometimes the best way to get into business is to buy an existing business. Be careful. Know what you are buying—do *due diligence*.

Due Diligence

The term *due diligence* is primarily used in conjunction with business acquisitions. It refers to the investigation that the buyer conducts to understand the business that is being purchased.

> **Landmine #27:** *Simply assume the seller of a business is lying, and you will have no surprises afterward.*

Whatever you are purchasing, it is necessary for you to do due diligence. It seems obvious, but it is shocking to see how many times acquisitions are made, both large and small, without the purchaser fully understanding what he or she is purchasing.

In a former corporate role that I had as the COO of a $1 billion (in sales) conglomerate, I watched as our company made a corporate acquisition for more than $100 million after doing only limited due diligence. Making matters worse, our board of directors who limited our time for due diligence, then made the CEO "guarantee" that our cash flow projections for the business being acquired were correct.

The acquisition was made through an investment bank auction process, whereby a large investment bank was handling the company sale and was soliciting offers through a bidding process.

The bids were to be made based on information provided by the investment banker in a "bid package" to prospective purchasers. The concept behind this approach is that the company being sold doesn't want to have multiple purchasers communicating with its management and staff, so a limited amount of information is accumulated and presented by the investment bankers in the "bid package." The bidders then are expected to rely on the information presented in the bid package and make their offers based on that information. The winning bidder is then afforded the opportunity to do <u>due diligence</u> to confirm the information in the bid package.

Our company submitted the winning bid. At that point, we were in a position to perform due diligence. I remember going into the CEO's office to discuss putting together a team of people to go to the company's corporate offices to really analyze and to some extent audit the company's records to make absolutely sure that we knew what we were buying.

This was a large acquisition and one of the major initiatives being pushed by our management team. I had a blank pad of paper and was ready for a long meeting. The CEO looked at me and asked, "Exactly what is the topic for this meeting?" Somewhat astonished, I responded, "Well, I had assumed, given our bid was accepted, that you would want to discuss putting together our team to do due diligence." Amazingly, the CEO informed me that given time constraints imposed by the Board that we were done with our due diligence. The CEO then rebuffed any further suggestions that we still needed to verify that the numbers provided by the investment bankers (upon which we had based our projections, valuation, and offer) were in fact correct.

As noted above, the CEO guaranteed the numbers, which were missed for the first quarter following the acquisition. The CEO lost his job over the entire affair.. I am not sure why the Board would not give us more time to verify the numbers further. I know that we had done a lot of work on the bid package and had a number of discussions with the management team, but again, that is not the same as really doing detailed analysis (i.e., due diligence).

The moral of the story is to know what you are buying and trust no one. Verify as much information as possible. Ask many questions; ask the same question of different people several times. Investigate any discrepancies, even when they may appear to be minor issues.

The level and type of due diligence needed depends heavily on the type of business, but there is one common thread for any effective due diligence plan. This can't-miss due diligence step can best be summarized as "follow the cash." Accounting statements, projections, budgets, and even tax returns can lie, but the bank statements don't. They show the business's deposits, which can be reconciled to revenues, and the payments, which can be reconciled to expenses and capital outlays. These reconciliations can be messy and difficult, but generally they provide the only way for you to truly know how the business is performing.

I suggest getting the monthly bank statements for at least the last eighteen months. The seller will only want to provide the last month or two but insist on getting at least a year's statements.

Asset versus Corporate Acquisitions

Generally, there are two types of acquisitions: "asset" and "corporate."

An "asset" deal is just what it sounds like—a purchase of assets. The assets being acquired must be clearly defined in terms of what is being purchased by the buyer and what is being retained by the seller. In an asset acquisition, the buyer may also be assuming certain liabilities, such as trade accounts payable, for example, or vacation pay for existing employees.

A "corporate" acquisition means that the purchaser is buying the legal entity that owns and operates the business, and assuming all of the liabilities of the entity, including those that may not be known, such as legal claims that may not yet have been asserted.

Most small business acquisitions are done as asset deals. Larger companies often do corporate acquisitions, like Hewlett Packard buying Compaq. I think the simple reason is that small businesspeople are more concerned about protecting their money, so they are reluctant to assume the liabilities of another company. Large corporate CEOs are playing with OPM (i.e., other people's money), so they seem more willing to take the risks associated with a corporate acquisition. Generally, public companies are audited, which arguably gives purchasers some comfort that the financial statements for the company that they are buying are in fact accurate.

Although safer for the buyer, asset deals are more complex and more difficult to complete. In an asset deal, unless provided otherwise, the employees will remain employees of the selling company. So if the buyer wants the employees to work for him or her after the acquisition date, specific provisions must be made for the new company to hire the employees. Compensation programs can be changed or carried over at the discretion of the buyer. Seniority and benefits can also be carried over or eliminated.

In a corporate sale, the purchaser simply buys the stock and hence gets the company, all of its business, and all of the assets and liabilities associated with those businesses. Employees automatically come along with a corporate acquisition because they work for the company being acquired.

Intangible Assets

It is important in an asset deal that "intangible assets" be addressed. Things like the name of the business, customer list, "goodwill" (term referring to the value of the ongoing business enterprise), websites, and similar items need to be included in the list of assets being acquired.

For either an asset or corporate acquisition, you need to consider whether a noncompete agreement from management of the seller is important.

> *When I was growing up, my parents had a lake house on a freshwater lake in southern Wisconsin, affectionately and simply called the "cottage" by my family. When my dad finally came into some money, we bought a beautiful Sea Ray speedboat from a marina that we drove by on our route from home to the cottage.*
>
> *The marina location was great, given it was on a major thoroughfare from Chicago into the lakes area in southern Wisconsin. The marina had an exclusive dealership for Sea Ray boats for this area of greater Chicagoland. Most people knew about it—not only because of its great location, but because it had a signature marketing approach that was really cool. It had a fancy Sea Ray speedboat mounted on a steel pedestal approximately forty feet in the air, towering above the store.*
>
> *I remember that after a number of years operating successfully, the owner of the Sea Ray dealership sold the business, including the exclusive dealership rights and the awesome store location and flying boat!*
>
> *The purchaser obviously did not get a noncompete from the seller because two blocks away, the seller opened a new marina and, yes, you guessed it, mounted a new boat forty feet in the air. He didn't have Sea Ray any more, but he did have the same great location and his signature flying boat. My guess is that he also had his same customers, most of whom likely found him in his new location two blocks from the old one!*

The moral of the story is that no matter what anyone tells you, get some kind of noncompete agreement from the people selling you the business. Keep it reasonable because over-the-top noncompete agreements—those that are too stringent and go on for too long—are routinely struck down by the courts.

Summary

Know what you are buying. The most reliable due diligence involves reviewing twelve to eighteen months of past bank statements for the business being acquired and reconciling the actual cash activity with the financial statements and tax returns that the seller has provided you. Purchasing assets is most common for small business acquisitions, but this approach requires that employees be separately addressed. Make sure to address intangibles as part of the assets being acquired. A noncompete agreement from the seller's management is also important.

13

He's My Friend, so We'll Be Good Partners

Many new businesses are formed with two or more owners, often family or friends. If there are to be multiple owners, it is critical that the relationship between the owners be thought out, discussed, and documented in detail up front before the business opens its doors and before too much money is spent. This is true whether the owners are related or have known each other for fifty years. It doesn't matter; do not short-cut this critical step.

For a *limited liability company* the relationship between the owners (called *members*) is documented in the *operating agreement*. For a *limited or general partnership* the relationship between the owners (called *partners*) is documented in the *partnership agreement*. Because most new small businesses are formed as *LLC*s, I will focus on operating agreements, but the basic issues discussed below are almost identical for both legal forms of *organization*.

This chapter by its nature is somewhat technical, but it is important for anyone looking to form a new LLC to at least have a rudimentary understanding of these issues. Although they are couched in *lotsa legalese*, the issues are really business issues, not legal issues.

Understand Your Governing Document

Again, for an _LLC_ this is the _operating agreement_.

I suggest that the owners of a new business do as much work as possible on their _operating agreement_ and then take the initial draft to their attorney for review. Even though most attorneys simply mark up existing documents from ones already in their system, they still charge for the preparation time and effort. By doing the initial drafts yourself and then hiring an attorney to review and give his or her comments, you may be able to save time and money. More importantly, the owners will understand what is in the agreements, rather than having them produced and then partially explained by legal counsel.

Don't fret; legal documents can in fact be written in English, and your attorney can add the appropriate legalese, where necessary. So as a homebuilder you can write your own limited warranty, and then your attorney can take your document and add additional key words and capitalize or put words into boldface where necessary.

Entrepreneurs planning to go this route should devote adequate time and effort to ensure a quality first draft because if the draft presented to the attorney is a disaster, he or she may actually end up billing more for making endless corrections. I suggest starting with a sample operating agreement from Legal Zoom or one of the other online legal document sites. Alternatively, just ask your attorney for a "sanitized" (names, addresses, and other identifying information removed) agreement that the owners can use as a guide in discussing and documenting their understanding and agreement on the various issues.

Entrepreneurs who are uncomfortable working on the actual wording for their _operating agreement_ can create an issues list for all of the owners to discuss in an outline format. Then they can use

Key Considerations for Any LLC

The important issues that must be addressed in putting together any _operating agreement_ are listed below. The decisions made regarding these issues will ultimately define how the owners (_members_) will work together in the new business.

The key issues that need to be addressed in the _governing document_ are:
- purpose of the business entity;
- owners and ownership shares;
- owner contributions, initial and ongoing, and dilution;
- amount and timing of distributions;
- allocation of taxable income (for partnerships and LLCs);
- _manager_ versus owner control (in other words, who's in charge of what);
- manager duties and compensation;
- limits on other activities; and
- divorce provisions.

Purpose

The purpose of the company should be clear and should relate to the business idea or concept, but a decision will still need to be made whether to narrowly limit the new entity to the specific business opportunity or make it more flexible.

> For Tony's Italian Foods, LP, Bruno and Tony needed to decide whether to limit its business purpose to just owning and operating Tony's Fine Italian Restaurant, or whether the company should be able to open additional restaurants or start other businesses under the same or different names. The men decided to define the business

purpose broadly to allow them to own and operate any food service–related businesses.

Sometimes the business purpose can be written very broadly, allowing the company to go into any business, including car dealerships, retail stores, stock speculation, mining, or whatever. My personal preference is to have a fairly limited business purpose, as the members can always amend the business purpose to make it broader, assuming that they want to expand into other businesses.

Owners and Ownership Shares

This part of the governing document is fairly simple and covers just what it says. The agreement should specifically state the names of the owners and list their addresses and their percentage ownership of the company. If the partnership is a limited partnership, each partner's status as either general or limited should be stated.

Owner Contributions, Initial and Ongoing, and Dilution

In this section of the agreement, the initial contributions to be made by each member and their timing should be specified. It should also be clear whether the contribution is to be made in cash or in property. For any property contributions, the value or method of valuation must be specified.

> *For our favorite Italian restaurant, the governing document noted that Bruno and Tony each contributed some property, while Bruno's mom contributed $25,000 in cash. The <u>contributions</u> were actually made as follows: Tony contributed kitchen equipment that Bruno agreed to value at $25,000. Bruno contributed computers and other office equipment that Tony agreed had a value of $25,000. Consequently, each partner was credited with $25,000 in <u>capital contributions</u>.*

He's My Friend, so We'll Be Good Partners

If Bruno and Tony had not been able to agree on the value of the kitchen equipment, they could have specified that a value opinion would be obtained from a reliable source to determine the final valuation. Tony would ultimately have adjusted his contribution amount up or down based on the outcome of the valuation.

Typically, but not always, the relative amount of the initial capital contributions is consistent with the ownership interest.

So since Bruno, Tony, and Bruno's mom all contributed $25,000, they each received a stated 33.33 percent ownership interest in Tony's Italian Foods, LP.

This is not always the case, and in fact there are many complicated permutations that can be explored with your attorney, if you think it worthwhile.

Usually the initial capital contributions are not a difficult issue to agree on because the partners usually discuss this early on. Potentially causing heartburn, however, is the issue of capital contributions after the initial _contributions_ are made. There are several options here: no future owner contributions can be required, certain specified amounts can be required at set dates, or unlimited capital contributions can be required as _capital_ is needed (probably never a good idea).

My preference is to try to estimate all start-up costs and initial operating deficits and have the members put up all of the needed capital up front. This ensures that the business has the cash needed to get started and to operate long enough to get to _break-even cash flow_.

Problems arise if things are worse than the owners think, and more capital is needed or the business will have to close. No owner wants to be in the position of having to meet (pay) endless *capital calls* (a term meaning requests for a _capital contribution_). On the other hand, owners never want to be in a situation where the business only needs another $5,000 to get over the hump (to get to break-even cash flow), but the other owners are unwilling to put up their shares.

There are two ways to deal with this circumstance: (1) dilution (dreaded by most) and (2) partner loans.

Let's take yet another look at *Tony's Fine Italian*.

The restaurant is struggling, and the company needs another $25,000 for the business to survive. Bank loans are not available, and no other source of cash can be found except additional contributions from the partners. Bruno and his mom are each willing to put up their one-third share of the $25,000, but Tony refuses because he doesn't have the money.

Since the operating agreement provided for dilution, Bruno and Mom will each put up one-half of the needed $25,000, bringing their total capital contributions to $37,500 each. Tony will put up no new cash, so his total capital contribution will remain at his original $25,000 investment.

Dilution results, as Bruno and Mom now own 37.5 percent of the partnership (since they now each have contributed $37,500 of the $100,000 total contributions), and Tony is reduced from one-third (33.33 percent) ownership to 25 percent (since he contributed $25,000 of the $100,000 total contributions). Tony's ownership was reduced under the dilution provisions because he did not put up his share of the capital call.

Some may feel that Tony was treated fairly since he still gets to own 25 percent of the company, even though he did not support the company in its time of need. My experience is that most people do not like dilution because they feel it allows rich partners to "squeeze out" small, poorer partners. This is not wholly untrue.

The alternative to dilution is to provide for partner loans. Although it has a similar economic effect to dilution, it is generally preferred by most owners, as the stated ownership share of partners does not change.

Let's assume that instead of providing for dilution the LP agreement for Tony's Italian Foods, LP, provides for partner loans when cash is needed. Rather than providing the needed $25,000 as additional capital contributions, Bruno and his mom loan the company the $25,000 as partner loans. This $25,000 loan, plus interest at 20 percent, must be repaid before any cash is distributed to any of the owners.

Usually the interest rate is very high (sometimes as much as 20 percent) to entice one or more of the partners to loan the needed money to the company. Remember, the company cannot survive without the additional capital. The operating agreement must also provide that partner loans plus interest are repaid before any distributions are made to the owners. Again, this is done to incent some of the partners to make these partner loans to the company.

The net economic effect of partner loans is similar, but people like loans better because they feel that they can't be "squeezed out" of their ownership position through dilution.

Amount and Timing of Distributions

Have you ever tried to pay for a car, piece of clothing, or flat-panel television with profits? It doesn't work. No one cares about your profits; they expect to be paid in cash (or a reasonable facsimile thereof).

> **Landmine #28:** *Your attorney may not understand this, but businesses can't distribute profits; they can only distribute cash.*

A critical point about distributions is that they need to be based on *cash flow*, not profits. Many times attorneys who are not real clear on the differences use GAAP (generally accepted accounting principles) profits or net income as a basis for distributions, rather than cash flow. This is wrong and must be avoided. Profits or net income cannot be distributed, only cash or net cash flow can. Don't let your attorney or partner or anyone else tell you otherwise, no matter how many times the person says he or she has done it that way in other agreements!

An actual example of how owners can get in trouble when using something other than net cash flow as a basis for distributions follows:

I was involved with two partners (really members, as it was an LLC) in a start-up company that had been in existence for about six months. Mike and I were really owner/managers, and the third partner, Michelle, was not very involved in the day-to-day business at the time. Instead, Michelle was to focus on opening up a new line of business for the company that would leverage off some of her existing, but unaffiliated, business operations.

After deferring the start-up of this new line for months, Michelle came to Mike and me and proposed the following:

"I want this new line of business to be completely separate from our other business and to be operated through a new joint venture. I will get 60 percent of the profits (she actually meant revenues) and will pay 50 percent of the costs. You two will get the rest."

When Mike discussed the proposal with Michelle, she explained that we were only really giving up 10 percent, so we shouldn't be too concerned. Hmmm...

Let's assume that this new line of business would have annual cash revenues of $1 million and cash expenses of $800,000, leaving net cash flow of $200,000 or 20 percent. The owner splits of net cash flow proposed by Michelle would be as follows:

	TOTAL	MICHELLE	MIKE & GARY
REVENUES	$1,000,000	$600,000 (60%)	$400,000 (40%)
EXPENSES	$800,000	$400,000 (50%)	$400,000 (50%)
CASH FLOW	$200,000	$200,000 (100%)	$0 (0%)

Interesting, isn't it, how this seemingly benign proposal results in Mike and me getting nothing, while Michelle nets the entire $200K in annual cash flow from the business? Making matters worse is that at less than a 20 percent margin, Mike and I actually lose money, while Michelle still makes money.

There are two lessons to be learned here. First, partner shares should always be based on net cash flow or some derivative of net cash flow or, even better, "distributable cash" (net cash flow, less reserves for upcoming debt payments, equipment purchases, or other significant cash needs). And second, partners should always split based on the bottom-line net cash flow, not the "top-line" (revenues) or any GAAP- or profit-oriented calculations. Your friendly neighborhood attorney may not get this right, so you need to pay close attention to the distribution section of the operating agreement.

The above example demonstrates why "Mr. Wonderful" (Kevin O'Leary) on the television show *Shark Tank* almost always proposes a "licensing fee" versus a share of ownership. Just like Michelle in my deal, Mr. Wonderful knows he makes more money getting paid on the top line (with a license fee calculated on sales) versus getting his fair share of the bottom (net cash flow)! Mr. O'Leary is not a billionaire by accident. Anytime he can get someone to pay him on sales, he knows he is way ahead.

The owners must decide on a distribution policy—when cash generated by the business will be distributed to the owners. Part of the decision depends on the owners' goals for the business. Are the owners looking to have the business generate enough cash internally to be used for expansion, or are they more interested in having cash distributed?

For a business that is focused on using cash for expansion, the owners may agree that cash generated by the business be retained unless the partners decide and agree on a cash distribution in the future.

Alternatively, the owners may decide that any cash not needed for operations should be distributed. For such a company, it is important for the owners to agree up front on a minimum level of cash that the business needs to hold for any problems or issues that may come up. So the distribution policy could provide that after retaining the first $30,000 in net cash flow, the company will distribute 95 percent of remaining net cash flow each quarter. If the business is seasonal, you may want to make allowances for the off-season.

Allocation of Taxable Income (for Partnerships and LLCs)

Even though I have significant accounting training, have passed the CPA exam, and have read hundreds of partnership and operating agreements, I must admit that I no longer understand the wording that the attorneys typically insert for this section. It seems to be completely tax driven, so like the tax code, it is unintelligible. Therefore, I wouldn't worry too much about this section.

Generally, taxable income or loss is going to be allocated to the owners in accordance with their ownership percentages. If contributions or distributions are done in different percentages for whatever reason, taxable income or losses may be specially allocated to offset part of the difference.

Manager versus Member Control

The issue is what authority the <u>LLC</u> <u>manager</u> has versus what actions require an ownership or member vote.

There are no typical scenarios here. The division of authority between the manager and owners needs to be based on the business circumstances. Certainly, the manager needs to be able to operate the business on a day-to-day basis without having to get owner approvals for every little decision. At the same time, owners must feel that the manager is operating the business in a manner that is consistent with the business plan and annual operating budget.

Typical decisions that require owner approval in a small business include the following:
- sale of all or substantially all of the assets of the business;
- admission of a new partner;
- real estate purchases and leases;
- purchases above a specified dollar amount;
- the annual operating budget, including staffing plans;
- company sale or merger;
- a move into a new line of business;
- executive management compensation programs;
- lawsuit filings; and
- bankruptcy filings.

Some readers may be wondering how this is relevant because all of the owners are going to be involved as managers too, so there is no need to focus on owner-versus-manager authority and control issues. This is a mistake because ownership shares can change over time, and new owners can be added in the future.

A main issue on authority and control is not to make things so tight that you prevent the business from being able to operate. Creating too stringent an approval process can hamstring the business before you even start. My bias is to permit timely decision making by the manager and to rely on other provisions to control consistently poor management.

Management Duties and Compensation

Who is going to be in charge? Who is going to do what? What compensation, if any, are the *owner/managers* going to take from the company for the work that they do? What about expenses incurred by the owner/mangers while doing work for the company?

Again, there are no right answers to any of these questions. Obviously, for a new business, there may not be enough *cash flow* to pay salaries to owner/managers, so realistic decisions must be made.

What is most important is that the owners discuss and agree on these issues up front, and that the *operating agreement* clearly reflects the outcome of these discussions.

> **Landmine #29:** *Assume nothing; instead insist that all owner/managers state in writing their roles and responsibilities, including how much cash they will invest in the business.*

If there is more than one *owner/manager*, there must also be dispute resolution provisions. Obviously, the divorce provisions provide the ultimate dispute resolution process, but I suggest that something short of that be added to the agreement. Maybe one owner/manager will be designated as the managing member, giving him or her the power to resolve any disputes between the other owner/managers.

My feeling is that arbitration and mediation provisions are okay, but they are sometimes too slow to be effective in resolving such disputes.

HE'S MY FRIEND, SO WE'LL BE GOOD PARTNERS

Limits on Other Activities
Regardless of whether you think it applicable at the time or not, the <u>operating agreement</u> must clearly specify whether an owner or manager can engage in other business activities. If yes, the agreement must also address whether such activities can be competitive with the business of the company.

Divorce—General
Steve Jobs got fired from his own company! While I was watching the movie *Jobs* with my wife, she paused the playback and said to me, "I don't get it. How can they fire him from his own company?" Fair question. The answer is that he effectively took in partners and somewhat unknowingly left himself exposed. Considering what happened to Jobs, you shouldn't be shocked when I say that the most important provisions of any operating or partnership agreement are those stipulating how the owners can split up—get a divorce! In short, you must understand how your partners can get rid of you—and you them.

> **Landmine #30:** *Before getting married to a business partner, a family member or otherwise, you must negotiate and provide for the divorce in writing.*

The best time to discuss divorce is when no one thinks it will be needed. Why? Because people are less concerned, less passionate about things when they think they are irrelevant. In the glow surrounding a new business start-up, the owners are often not thinking or worried about divorce provisions. Rather, they are focused on the business and dreaming of how much money they are going to make. That makes it the perfect time to complete this critical step.

The basic options for business divorces that I have seen used are as follows:
- "shotgun" or "buy/sell";
- partner right to sell ownership to a third party;
- forced company sale; and
- put or calls.

You will need to get legal advice on the intricacies of each of these provisions. The discussion that follows is solely to familiarize you with the basic concepts and how they work, so that you can effectively manage your attorney.

Divorce—Shotgun

A "shotgun" or buy/sell provision is extremely effective, albeit scary. It is also probably the most fair and most expeditious method of getting a business divorce. It can be easily summarized as one side cuts the pie and the other picks the piece. Specifically, with a shotgun provision, one side names the price for an ownership interest in the business and lets the other partner decide whether to buy or sell at that price.

Consider an example from our hypothetical business, *Tony's Fine Italian:*

Things are not going well at Tony's. The business is barely surviving, and fewer and fewer customers are coming in every day. Bruno has called several member (owner) meetings—no one is drinking beer at the meetings anymore!—and he and Tony cannot agree on how to address the business's problems. Tony wants to invest in new kitchen equipment, which he thinks will improve the quality of the food and bring in more customers. Bruno is convinced that the restaurant needs a new and better chef, or the business will fail. Tony insists that their agreement was that he would be chef, which in fact, it was. But Bruno felt misled because Tony said he was a trained, quality chef, but he is a short-order cook at best.

HE'S MY FRIEND, SO WE'LL BE GOOD PARTNERS

Bruno reviews the operating agreement and reads the "buy/sell" provisions. He invokes the buy/sell ("shotgun") and names a price of $50,000. Tony now must decide whether to buy Bruno out for the $50,000 or sell his entire ownership to Bruno for the named price.

See what I mean—scary! Since Bruno wants to stay involved with the restaurant, he can't name a price that is too low, or Tony will exercise his right to buy. Therefore, Bruno must name a price that he feels that Tony will sell at, which forces him to name a price that is relatively high.

It galls Bruno to pay this boob and former friend $50,000 to get rid of him, especially given the fact that Tony only invested $25,000. Assuming he sells, Tony will actually make money for doing nothing but screwing things up miserably! Since Bruno has already been talking with a new chef, Alfred, who he feels strongly will get the restaurant moving in the right direction, he feels justified naming a premium price to help ensure that Tony will sell. At this point, Bruno just wants to buy Tony out and move forward with his plans.

My personal experiences in invoking shotgun provisions, both times as buyer, both resulted in positive outcomes. The biggest gain came when a company that I was president of had a partnership with a Japanese construction company that owned land.

The partnership owned a beautiful white-sand beachfront development site divided into four separate parcels. The partnership was structured as a fifty-fifty deal (almost always a bad idea).

My company wanted to proceed with development of one of the four land parcels. After spending a year or more on planning and analysis, I decided that the highest (most profitable) and best use for the first parcel was for a time-share resort.

I offered our Japanese partner the option to either (1) sell its 50 percent ownership in this parcel to my company so we could proceed with the development or (2) stay on as a partner and jointly develop the time-share resort (we had already identified an experienced time-share company to partner with on the time-share sales and marketing).

After over a year of meetings in Tokyo, Honolulu, Maui, and Las Vegas, the Japanese partner refused to make a decision. Even though my company was the managing partner, our business plans were effectively stymied by the fact that the Japanese partner's 50 percent ownership gave it veto power.

The good news was that the partnership agreement had a shotgun provision. However, the provision could not be applied to one parcel of land; it could only be applied to the entire ownership interest of a partner, effectively to all four parcels. After significant deliberation, I was able to convince my board of directors to invoke the shotgun, which was done at a price of $30 million.

The Japanese partner balked at first, feeling insulted that we no longer wanted to be partners, but eventually it complied with the terms of the shotgun and sold its entire ownership interest in all four parcels to us for the stated $30 million price. One year later, we sold just the first parcel to a well-known, branded hotel/time-share company for $65 million.

The point is that using the shotgun provision was the only way that our company could move forward with the business on that land parcel. Again, it can be a very effective tool in ending a dysfunctional partnership. I know—your company will never become dysfunctional, but put in the shotgun anyway, Humor me!

Divorce—Partner Right to Sell Ownership to Third Party

In many agreements, there is a "lockout" period during which no owner can sell or transfer his or her ownership interest. This is typically done to ensure that owner issues do not get in the way of

He's My Friend, so We'll Be Good Partners

a new business trying to establish itself. Usually, it is not a bad idea for a year or two.

In my opinion, at some point the partners need to be afforded the ability to sell their ownership interest. The problem is that for a small business there typically are not very many potential buyers, if any. Furthermore, small businesses are usually difficult to value. Compounding matters further, a minority interest in a business usually has less value than a majority or controlling interest. Finally, when a partner wants to sell his or her interest to a third party that is a competitor, a whole host of additional issues and concerns are raised. These issues need to be discussed by the owners and addressed in the operating agreement.

The provision that I prefer here is what is commonly called a "*right of first offer*." Very simply, this gives any owner the right to sell, but before going to market, he or she must offer to sell to the other owners. The other owners are not obligated to buy or even make an offer, but they are given the opportunity. The nonselling owners can make a written offer to the owner who wants to sell. The selling owner can either then accept the nonselling owner's offer or go to market and try to sell at a higher price. The selling owner cannot sell at a price below what the nonselling owners offered but is free to sell at a higher price.

My feeling is that a right of first offer provides a fair balance between giving the nonsellers a chance to buy and the seller a chance to get a decent, fair price for his or her ownership interest. This option can be coupled with a restriction that no sale can be made to a competitor, which I think is a good idea.

Forced Sale

Given the difficulties of selling a minority interest in any small business, some owners agree that if any owner or group of owners wants to sell, they can force a sale of the entire company. This tends to maximize the selling price but, of course, leaves owners who want to continue with the business in the difficult position of having to bid against other potential buyers for their own business.

Put or Call Options

Owners can be given the right to "put" their interest to the other owners, which just means that the other owners must buy out the owner who puts his or her interest. Many times the put price is at a discount or is just return of capital as it forces owners to buy when they may not want to buy at the time.

A call is the opposite of a put. A call option gives certain owners the right to purchase another owner's interest. Since the owner may not want to sell, the call price is often at a premium to value (higher than true fair market value) or can only be triggered under certain circumstances.

Summary

Your company's operating or partnership agreement, the governing document, sets the <u>ground rules</u> for how you are going to operate. It is not something that your attorney drafts and you don't even read because you're too busy working on other aspects of launching your business—really, really a bad idea. Rather, it is a document that every business owner must read and understand. It is definitely an agreement that can be written in plain English, so you can understand it—except, of course, the profit-and-loss allocation section discussed above, which is now based on the IRS code.

Be sure to cover "divorce" very specifically in the operating or partnership agreement.

14

MY EMPLOYEES WILL LOVE ME

Your employees don't need to love you, just respect and trust you. You earn respect and trust by being honest and trusting them. Treat your employees like partners—tell them what you are thinking, ask for their input. Share the business's problems and challenges with key employees; don't try to hide things from them. When you try to hide difficulties, the employees know it, and they lose confidence in you.

Lead; be a leader. The best way to lead is to make decisions and make them quickly. Employees hate bosses who can't make decisions; it leaves them in limbo, not knowing exactly how to proceed. Even worse than not making a decision is making a decision and then reversing it almost immediately. I am not suggesting that you continue implementing a decision that proves to be wrong, but I am suggesting that when you make a decision you stick with it until it is proven wrong. When you change direction, you need to explain to your staff why you made the original decision and why you now need to change direction.

A real-life example of how to completely alienate your employees and partners follows:

New Business Landmines

I was in a partnership with three other partners based in Lake Tahoe. All of the partners were owner/managers, and I was actually at the bottom of the totem pole as far as authority in the partnership. At a partner meeting, the managing partner decided that we should open a telemarketing center in Chicago, where I lived (this was before "do-not-call-list" laws were passed). The reasoning was that office space and employees were readily available in Chicago, and even though I was no expert in managing a telemarketing center, having me in an office there would add some oversight and control.

Being a hard worker and good partner, I immediately started meeting with commercial real estate brokers and looking for office space. I also engaged legal counsel to make sure that we were dealing with any licensing and regulatory issues (telemarketing was and is heavily regulated). In addition, I started working on staffing and recruiting plans. Finally, being a financial guy, I started preparing my start-up-cost budget and monthly cash flow projections.

After working for about six weeks, I had identified and negotiated a lease, and I had addressed the regulatory and business issues. I prepared a complete plan for an upcoming partnership meeting on how we would proceed. To my astonishment, when I started to present the plan to the partners, the managing partner stopped me and asked, "Why are we even talking about this? I made the decision a month ago not to proceed with the Chicago telemarketing center."

As a postscript, I later found that the same managing partner had also signed a three-year lease for a telemarketing center in Springfield, Missouri. We never even moved into the space, and I had to negotiate a lease termination and settlement agreement after the managing partner was finally pushed out of the organization!

Who Are You?

What kind of manager are you? It's important to know, don't you think?

I know that I think through numbers. I need to take an idea, sit down in front of a computer, and crank out the potential economics (financial pros and cons) to evaluate it. It's just how I think.

How about you? How do you think? What are your strong and weak points?

What kind of supervisor/manager are you? Are you detailed? Are you comfortable telling people face-to-face what they are doing wrong? Can you do so professionally—even when someone has cost you a sale or a customer?

All <u>owner/managers</u> must evaluate their own managerial strengths and weaknesses honestly and then compare them to the needs of their new business. It is possible that you may have the greatest business idea ever. You may even be the right person to put together the business plan, raise the necessary <u>capital</u>, and launch the business. However, you may be the worst person on the planet to manage the day-to-day business after it is born!

Maybe you are an owner, but you are not the right manager.

Landmine #31: *You may not be the best person to run your own business!*

Don't worry; I am not trying to cut you out of your own deal, but I do want to challenge every entrepreneur to honestly evaluate his or her strengths and weaknesses. If you can't think of any weaknesses, ask someone to help you. If you are married, I know that you can get a list of weaknesses from your spouse!

Then, separately, write down what key managerial skills you think are needed to (1) launch the business and (2) manage the business day-to-day. Now compare the lists and be honest with yourself. Are you the best person to run your business? Do the same for your partners. Where do their skills fit? Are the strengths and weaknesses of the entire management team complementary or duplicative?

In considering your roles in the business and your staffing needs, this analysis is critical.

Some businesses require a "hands-off," laissez-faire approach to managing employees. Other businesses require that employees be supervised closely and constantly. Where does your business fit? Again, match the business needs with the management team's strengths. If the business's needs are not met by the owner/manager's skills, then consider alternatives, including hiring supervisors to handle the business's requirements.

Who's Boss?

Everything seems important when the business starts. Regardless, some things are more important than others. Every manager must find a way to prioritize his or her time and focus on the things that are most important. The struggle is how to do that—how not to get bogged down in endless details and how not to let your employees (beloved or not) and smartphone dictate your priorities and schedule.

> **Landmine #32:** *Stop answering your phone every time it rings, and that applies to texts and e-mails too!*

To start, you must make a pact with your smartphone. You are its boss, not the other way around. You must not pick up every call when the phone rings—period. If you do, the smartphone controls you—it is boss. So take control and let it ring, especially when you are in a meeting with an employee.

I was an accounting manager and was meeting with a tax partner from my firm, meaning that I was lower on the totem pole. Normally, in a meeting between a partner and a manager, if the manager's phone rang, the manager let it ring. However, if the partner's phone rang, he interrupted the meeting and picked up the call.

However, in one meeting with this certain tax partner, the partner's phone rang, and I said, "Oh, go ahead and get that. I'll wait." To which the tax partner responded, "I'll tell you what, why don't you go over to that phone over there and call me, and then we can have an uninterrupted meeting. No, I'll let it ring. There is no reason for me to interrupt my meeting with you (in person) because my phone is ringing."

Wow! I will never forget that—and from a tax accountant! Maybe he was reading a Tom Peter's book or something because he knew who the boss of his phone was! I can't tell you how many people I have worked for who let the telephone control them and their time. A successful <u>owner/manager</u> starts by taking control of his or her smartphone. Use it; don't let it use you!

Three Squares

Next, I suggest eating. Yep, I think <u>owner/managers</u> can run a more successful business if they eat three squares a day. I know this seems crazy, but hear me out on this one. There is not a much more social interaction for human beings than sharing a meal together. So as an <u>owner/manager</u>, take time to eat; it will create opportunities for people—employees, partners, vendors, customers—to eat with you, and for you to decompress with them and maybe get to know them.

Can you discuss business while you eat? Assuming you are not in the waste disposal business, sure, of course. Other discussion topics can and will come up too. Eating makes people seem more human to staff and others, so eat. Yes, it is a priority!

I had a boss once who was an attorney with really poor people skills. This was partly due to the boss being a real nerd and partly due to him being extremely intelligent. He was known around the office as an idiot savant, mostly because he had zero common sense, but all recognized his high intellect.

At some point, someone had told this boss about his impersonal, somewhat cool managerial style. To compensate, the savant would start every meeting by asking "How is your family?"

The first few times the boss asked, I assumed his question was nice and genuine. However, because he asked the same question meeting after meeting, almost as a ritual, the question and answer became obligatory. This obviously negated the boss's attempts at trying to improve his interpersonal skills.

After sharing a few lunches or breakfasts, people can start to get to know one another at a personal level, and trust can start to build. Eat and take someone with you.

Priorities

Okay, so you control your phone, and you eat. What are your next priorities? If you aren't sure, I suggest that you pull out your rolling twelve-week cash forecast and review it. My guess is that you will end up looking at the sales line and will be most apprehensive about whether it's achievable. Assuming that is the case, your priorities will be marketing and sales. In the end, only you can set the priorities. Just know that you will likely get pushed and pulled in many directions, and that there will be many demands on your time. You must learn to say "no" or at least "not now."

I wish I could prescribe a definitive way to manage your time, but really I have not found any one method that works. I can tell you that I know when I am wasting my time—when I am spending time on something that is not "getting the cash," as my old boss and friend advised. When I find myself in those situations now, I try as hard as possible without being a complete ass to extricate myself. Sometimes you just need to make an excuse so you can get back to making money.

Here are a few ad hoc suggestions that I think may help some:
- Prepare written agendas for meetings.
- Return phone calls at a set time in the morning and afternoon.
- Set time limits on meetings with employees.
- Be a good listener.
- Keep it light and laugh a little, even in the face of adversity; people will respect you for it.

Sometimes people try to steer clear of conflict or confrontations, and they will use meetings, phone calls, and other diversions to avoid having to address "real issues." This can lead to disaster. Most employees want clear and unchanging direction. There is nothing worse than a boss who will not address difficult issues because he or she is nonconfrontational. You must not fall into this trap. Instead you must make decisions and communicate them clearly to your employees.

Delegation

Delegation is an important potential time-saver. Obviously, you need someone you can trust to delegate anything of importance. Unfortunately, these types of people are not easy to find, but if you find some, keep them because they can be irreplaceable. Knowing how much and when to delegate is more art than science. There are no hard-and-fast rules. Trial and error can be effective. Often <u>owner/managers</u> are so busy that they feel it is just quicker and easier to do "it" themselves. I can appreciate this sentiment, but it is a trap. Owner/managers who do not delegate leave themselves in the ongoing position of being the only ones able to perform the task, whatever it is. For this reason, *owner/mangers* must take the time to train and delegate.

Summary

Match the owner/mangers' skills with the skills needed to best manage the new business. Know the strengths and weaknesses of the managers and try to ensure that the roles and responsibilities make sense. Set priorities for each day and manage your time. Take control of the smartphone and your schedule.

15

WHAT DOES IT ALL MEAN?

There are so many different things to take care of when starting and managing a new business. Sometimes the amount of work can feel overwhelming. In this book I have tried to provide guidance on how to best complete the most important tasks and avoid the "landmines" that can trip up any entrepreneur. Avoiding these "landmines" and keeping your priorities straight are critical to your success.

It is important to commit the time necessary to succeed but also to take some time off. Part of the reason I suggest entrepreneurs eat three meals a day is because it will create at least three breaks from working. However, you may need more. I know that sometimes being away from your business for a couple of days or even a week can lead to a different perspective when you return. A different perspective can then allow an *owner/manager* to more clearly see solutions to problems that may have seemed intractable in the past.

I encourage you to take the plunge, as I told my brother, and become your own boss—an entrepreneur. The good news is that owner/managers usually control their schedules; the bad news is that they work endless hours in pursuit of achieving their business goals. My wife once remarked, "Gary doesn't work 24-7, but he could be working anytime 24-7," which I think was a wise observation. There is no such thing as "business hours" when you are an entrepreneur. Owner/managers work when they have to, not when someone else tells them to. The smart ones only work when they are productive.

I sincerely hope that your new business venture meets your expectations, and that this book helps you avoid the landmines that can keep you from succeeding. If I can help in any way, please feel free to e-mail me at garyg@GoQBO.com.

ABOUT THE AUTHOR

<u>Gary Grottke</u>

Gary has started almost a dozen new businesses—some for himself and some for others. However, he didn't start out as an entrepreneur. His educational background and initial work experience were financially oriented. He received an undergraduate degree in economics from Vanderbilt University and a master's in accounting from Purdue University. He passed the CPA exam in 1980 and practiced in public accounting with a large firm for nine years. His father, grandfather, aunt, sister, and brother were or are all accountants and auditors. As you might guess, he tends to look at the world through the lens of numbers. He believes that there is no better background than accounting for becoming an entrepreneur and business owner.

Although his background is financial, Gary has mostly held managerial positions in corporate America, where he worked for almost twenty years before becoming an entrepreneur. During his career he worked with:
- agribusiness, manufacturing, and branded food products;
- heavy-equipment dealerships;
- hotels and time-share resorts;
- department stores;
- restaurants and park concessions;

- golf courses;
- home building;
- property management; and
- land and property development.

Much of Gary's exposure to these various businesses was as the chief operating officer of a $1 billion conglomerate. Obviously, he spent more time on some business segments than others, but he gained exposure to many types of businesses.

Since moving out of corporate America, he has started and managed businesses ranging from financial consulting, to home building, to time-share resort development and sales, to loan packaging, and to marketing and selling travel products.

Gary is currently CEO of Business Kickoff and Quality Back Office, two sister companies that assist entrepreneurs and small businesses in getting started and in managing their business back-office functions once they are up and operating.

EXHIBIT A

DEFINITIONS OF BUSINESS JARGON

"*Annual Report*" is a short-form report filed with the secretary of state's office annually for any type of company. It usually requires payment of a small fee, often a couple hundred dollars.

"*Break-even cash flow*" is when monthly cash receipts equal or slightly exceed monthly cash disbursements. It is a critical milestone for any new business and usually signifies a point when the business has a more secure future.

"*Capital*" is the total of the *equity capital* and the loans to the business. For example if the owners put $100,000 into the business and the business secures a $200,000 loan, the total capital for the business is $300,000.

"*Capital contributions*" are cash and property contributed to a company by the owners.

"*Capitalization*" is a term that refers to the capital structure for the business.

"*Cash Flow*" is cash receipts, less cash disbursements for any period of time.

"*Contributions*" means the same as *capital contributions*.

"_Collateral_" is generally used in reference to a loan. Collateral are assets of the borrower that are used by the lender to justify making the loan. Lenders look at collateral as something that if the business fails can be sold to raise cash to pay off the loan. Collateral typically includes real estate, stocks or bonds, vehicles, equipment, inventory, or accounts receivables. A lender may want to take a _security interest_ (e.g., a mortgage on real estate) in the borrower's collateral to ensure that it can't be sold by the borrower without the lender approving the sale.

"_Cost plus pricing_" refers to pricing your product or service at its actual cost, plus a certain percentage added onto the costs.

"_Debt-to-equity ratio_" is simply a ratio as stated of debt (or loans) to _equity capital_. If a company has a $200,000 loan relative to $100,000 in _equity capital_, the debt to equity ratio would be 2:1

"_Due diligence_" refers to the investigation that a buyer does to understand the business that he or she is buying. It is not a full audit but can include one. Its goal is to determine a fair value for the business based on its future prospects.

"_Equity_" means the same as _equity capital_.

"_Equity capital_" represents cash and property that are contributed or put into the business by the owners, both owner/managers and investors.

"_FFE_" means furniture, fixtures, and equipment.

"_Governing document_" refers to a legal agreement between the owners of a company that provides the ground rules for how the company will be owned and operated.

"_Investors_" means people or companies who invest or put cash or property in the company but who are not involved in management. Their investment maybe characterized as either a loan or as equity (ownership). Typically, a bank or finance company that

DEFINITIONS OF BUSINESS JARGON

loans money to the business is not called an investor, but an individual who loans money to the business can sometimes be referred to as an investor.

"*Investment capital*" this refers to the cash and property that the owners (whether they be owner/managers or investors) put into the business. This money is there to launch and sustain the business until it can start to generate enough cash flow to cover all of its operating costs and expenses.

"*Legalese*" means lawyerly words or legal jargon.

"*Limited Liability Company*" or "*LLC*" is a legal entity that is used by many owner/managers to own and operate their business. It must be registered with the state, which can typically be done on the Internet.

"*Loan-to-value*" is a simple ratio of the amount of any loan to the value of the collateral for the loan. So if purchasing a building for $500,000 with a $400,000 loan, the loan-to-value or "LTV" would be 80 percent (calculated as $400,000 loan divided by the $500,000 building value).

"*Lotsa*" is a highly technical term meaning a real lot of something. One of Gary's few "take-aways" from graduate school.

"*Marketing mix*" refers to the combination of different advertising and promotional programs employed by the business to market its products or services.

"*Manager*" in the context of an *LLC* means the person who has the responsibility to manage the affairs of the LLC. The duties and powers of the manager are defined in the *operating agreement* and can be very broad or very narrow.

"*Members*" is a term that means the owners of an *LLC*. The owners or *members* can be either *owner/managers* or *investors*.

"*Net worth*" means the difference between the total assets and total liabilities for a person or company.

"_Nondisclosure or Noncircumvention Agreement_" a legal agreement whereby a person receiving a business plan or other confidential information from another person agrees to keep such information confidential and not use such information for his or her own benefit. These agreements are often difficult to enforce, but are not a bad idea when sharing propriety plans and ideas with other people.

"_NDA_" means a "Nondisclosure Agreement"

"_Operating Agreement_" is the governing document for an _LLC_ that describes the relationship between the owners and how they will do business together.

"_Optimize_" slang for _SEO_.

"_Organized_" is used when referring to setting up the company to own and operate the business. The company that will own and operate the business can be a sole proprietorship, partnership, _limited liability company_ or corporation. These alternate forms for organizing the business are described in chapter 4.

"_Owner/manager_" refers to a person who both owns all or a portion of a business and who is also actively involved in the day-to-day a management of the business. There can be more than one owner/manager for any business.

"_Partners_" refers to the owners of a partnership and can be ether general (involved in day-to-day management) or limited (passive investors).

"_Partnership Agreement_" is the governing document for a partnership that describes the relationship between the _partners_ and how they will do business together.

"_Personal financial statements_" or "_PFS_" means a listing of a person's primary assets (e.g., cash, stocks, 401K accounts, houses, cars, jewelry, etc.), liabilities (e.g., credit card balances, mortgage loans, car loans, student loans, etc.), and _net worth_ prepared as of a certain date.

"_Personal guarantee_" is an agreement to pay the liability of another person or company made by an individual.

"_Right of First Offer_" refers to an agreement whereby an owner who wants to sell his or her interest in a company must first give the other owners the option to make an offer to purchase his interest. The selling owner is then free to either sell to the other owners or to a third party as long as they pay more than the other owner's offer.

"_Ripe_" is our term that refers to when a lawsuit is ready for a settlement offer.

"_Search engine optimization_" *or* "_SEO_" refers to the process of designing a website so that it will come up high in a "Google search."

"_Security interest_" refers to legal documents that give a lender rights to some or all of the proceeds from the sale of _collateral_.

"_Working capital_" technically means cash, receivables, and inventory less accounts payables and other short-term liabilities. In the context of this book, I usually mean cash.

EXHIBIT B1

SAMPLE BUSINESS PLAN (NARRATIVE ONLY)

Executive Summary

Freddy Smith (the "Principal"), a licensed general contractor with thirty-five years' experience in real estate construction and sales will raise $1 million in investment capital to purchase, renovate, and sell residential properties. Property Management by Smith, LLC (the "Company") will purchase properties in the far western suburbs of Atlanta, including Centerville and Clear Lake and the surrounding suburbs.

The Principal hopes to take advantage of the current real estate market that includes a number of distressed sales and bank-owned properties that are being sold at heavily discounted prices. Smith believes, based on direct observation of market conditions, that once these properties are renovated that they can be sold at a substantial profit margin (averaging 40 percent).

The timing for this business opportunity appears to be ideal given the local real estate market seems to have finally flattened after declining significantly from its 2008 peak.

SAMPLE BUSINESS PLAN (NARRATIVE ONLY)

The Principal plans to provide general contracting services for the Company's properties for a market-based fee. All accounting, administration, and tax services will also be outsourced, so the Company will not need to have any employees, and overhead costs will be kept to a minimum.

Investors will receive a minimum return of 6 percent before Smith can share in distributions from net sale and financing proceeds. The Principal will receive a 20 percent share of distributions, assuming the investors are current on their minimum return. The term of the investment shall not exceed forty-eight months, and the Company will not purchase any new properties after the thirtieth month.

The cash flow projections reflect a 33.5 percent IRR on the investors' money and a doubling of their investment in thirty-six months. This is predicated on the purchase, renovation, and sale of twenty-one properties. Seven of the properties are assumed to be rented and financed before their ultimate sale. The actual number of properties purchased and rented can vary significantly, depending on market conditions and economic factors.

There are a number of business risks that are summarized in the business plan that follows.

Description of Business

The Company's primary business will be to purchase, renovate, and sell residential properties. In some cases, the Company will rent a property before selling it to generate income. The Company expects that most or all of its purchases will be single-family houses but reserves the right to purchase condominiums or town houses, assuming conditions warrant.

The Company will focus its activities in Atlanta's far western suburbs where the Principal has significant experience, including (but not limited to) Centerville, Oswego, Plainfield, Yorkville, and Clear Lake. Generally, the Company will look to purchase houses that are being sold under distress such as "short sales," bank REO sales, and other forced sales. It is anticipated that the purchase prices paid for each individual property will be in the range of $50,000 to $225,000. All purchases will be completed with cash—no financing unless there is attractive seller financing. As such, properties will be owned free and clear with no encumbrances.

Prior to consummating the purchase of any property, the Principal will inspect the property and prepare a preliminary list of renovation costs ("Prelim Reno Budget"). The Prelim Reno Budget will have a 10 percent cost-contingency line item. The Principal will also undertake and document a market analysis to determine (1) whether the purchase price for each property is reasonable and (2) whether the projected selling price for each property after renovation will result in at least a 20 percent profit margin. The Company will not acquire any properties unless the projected profit margin on the purchase, renovation and sale > 20 percent.

For all purchased properties, the Principal will act as the general contractor for all renovations and will charge a 20 percent general contracting fee calculated on "Hard Costs" (i.e., all renovation costs, including carpentry, painting, carpet, roofing, permitting fees, siding, etc., but not including any design or architectural fess, insurance, interest, or similar expenses). Definitive written quotes will be obtained for all material and subcontractor costs prior to beginning work. The Prelim Reno Budget will then be updated to arrive at a final renovation cost budget ("Final Reno Budget"). Lien waivers will be obtained concurrent with making any payment to a subcontractor or material provider. Depending on the

SAMPLE BUSINESS PLAN (NARRATIVE ONLY)

scope of work, most renovations will take anywhere from two to six months, most will be two to four months.

The Company anticipates purchasing properties for the first thirty months after formation using available funds (from both investor contributions and from net proceeds from sales or financings), and that all properties, including those rented, will be sold no later than forty-eight months after formation. As such, the Company may own twelve or more properties at any one time and may have up to six properties under renovation at any one time.

Builder's Risk and Property & Liability Insurance will be obtained for all properties. Insurance certificates will be obtained from all material providers and subcontractors consistent with industry practice. The Company will also maintain an E & O insurance policy.

All properties will be sold without warranty, except that manufacturer warranties will be assigned to the buyers at closing.

It is anticipated that properties will be listed for sale with local realtors. The Company's target profit margin is 40 percent on all house sales, but the actual margin may vary significantly from property to property. The Company hopes to be able to negotiate a lower commission than market given the volume of houses that it will be listing and selling. However, the Company will only reduce the listing broker's commission; the commission for the buyer's broker will not be reduced. The Company believes that offering lower commissions to buyers' brokers can reduce showings and hence slow sales. The Company may also try to sell some properties without realtors. For these properties, the Company will be willing to pay a buyer's broker commission, again to encourage showings. When advantageous to the Company, the Company may use dual agents—agents representing both buyer and seller.

For certain properties, including those that do not sell quickly, the Company may elect to rent the property. This decision will be based on market conditions at the time and for the property. Rental rates will be at market. In some cases, real estate brokers/agents may be used to locate and qualify tenants. Leasing fees for such services typically are one month's rent on a one-year lease. The Company will seek to take at least one month's rent as a security deposit. Generally, the Company will only enter into a one-year lease, but there may be circumstances where shorter duration leases are advantageous to the Company. Generally, rental rates in the area range from $700 to $2,100, depending on the size and location of the property (the Principal believes the current market rental rate is $1.17/sf).

The Company may also enter into lease to buy contracts, which may include longer lease terms. These contracts may result in even higher rents when buyers are unable to obtain mortgage financing as they may end up forfeiting excess amounts paid toward the purchase price.

Tenant security deposits will be maintained in a separate bank account and will not be used for corporate purposes.

For any properties that the Company decides to rent, the Company may decide to finance the property. It is anticipated that the loan-to-value on such financing will be in the 50 to 70 percent range. Financing terms are subject to negotiation with the lenders, but commercial terms today typically require monthly payments based on a twenty-year amortization schedule, 6 percent interest, first mortgage on property, and a maturity date in three to five years. Company principals may be required to guarantee the loan. In such cases, loan guarantee fees may apply equal to .25 percent quarterly of the amount guaranteed.

SAMPLE BUSINESS PLAN (NARRATIVE ONLY)

The *Cash Flow Projection* attached as <u>Exhibit A</u> *(not included)* provides an example of the potential timing and results for property purchases, renovations, rentals, financings, and sales. Changes in various assumptions are reflected on the Summary of Cash Flow Sensitivities attached as <u>Exhibit B</u> *(not included)*.

The Company will be a limited liability company, member-managed by Freddy Smith (the "Principal"), who will not receive a salary. All renovation work will be handled by the Principal, a licensed general contractor, pursuant to a contract between the Company and the Principal. All accounting, tax, and administrative services will be outsourced to Quality Back Office Solutions ("QBO").

Management Team
Patrick, Sr. and Jane Smith

Patrick's father, Leroy Smith, began Smith Construction as a renovation and remodeling company in the mid-1950s. Patrick ran sales and field operations, and Jane handled the administrative responsibilities. for Smith Construction. Patrick assumed the reins when Leroy retired in 1985. Smith Construction grew to be one of the largest residential builders in the Atlanta area under Patrick and Jane's supervision until they decided to sell the company in 2003.

Jane has expertise in accounting, office administration, and scheduling, while Patrick has expertise in property evaluation and construction. Patrick's ability upon initial inspection to ascertain market value and price needed repairs will enable them to achieve the desired high profit results needed for this operation.

Patrick and Jane are licensed general contractors in the state of Georgia. They have twenty-eight years of experience in residential building and renovation in the target market area.

Harvey Smith, Project Operations
Harvey has been involved in the family business since he was a young boy cleaning job sites for his father. He has twenty years of experience as a construction management professional, offering skilled experience in sales, estimating, project management, project controls, project finance, safety, and scheduling. Harvey earned his bachelor's degree at Alabama State College in construction management. Harvey has experience working for several large home builders as a project manager. Harvey is detailed, organized, and experienced in managing all trades for multiple large projects at once.

Patrick M. Smith, Jr., Advisor
Patrick has been involved in the family home building, remodeling, and real estate investment business for most of his life. Shortly after receiving his bachelor's degree from University of Georgia in 1995, Patrick earned his real estate license. He spent several years successfully leading sales and marketing efforts for Smith Construction as well as other builders. In 2002, Patrick left the real estate industry and took a position with Ford Motor Co while earning an MBA in accounting at Clear Lake University.

Gary Grottke, Financial Advisor
Mr. Grottke has over thirty years financial and real estate experience. He is a CPA and a licensed general contractor in Illinois. He has a BA from Vanderbilt University and an MBA from Purdue University. His work experience includes a decade at KPMG Peat Marwick, twelve years managing a large land development company in Hawaii, and eleven years in various entrepreneurial ventures, including building custom homes in Wheaton and Glen Ellyn.

SAMPLE BUSINESS PLAN (NARRATIVE ONLY)

Mr. Grottke's services are brought to the Company through the *QBO Services Agreement*. He is owner and manager of QBO, which is a financial services firm offering "turnkey" back-office services to businesses throughout the United States. Mr. Grottke's firm will handle all accounting, bill paying, lien waiver processing, administration, maintenance of property records and files, investor reporting and communications, and tax compliance for the Company.

Investment Details

The Company will raise $1 million from various investors. The Company will accept investments in amounts not less than $50,000, subject to the discretion of the Principal. Each investor will initially enter into a nonbinding letter of interest, specifying his or her interest in making an investment.

Once the Company has gathered *Letters of Interest* aggregating $1 million, the Company will proceed with formation and preparation of the definitive Subscription Agreements. The Subscription Agreements will provide for the following:

- Investors will receive a preferred return of 6 percent on the outstanding investment balance, paid quarterly;
- Company can use any and all available cash resources, including net sales and refinancing proceeds to purchase houses for thirty months. After thirty months, the Company will not purchase any more properties;
- Assuming investors are current on their preferred return and assuming company projections reflect that the investors will receive all of their investment back, plus at least their 6 percent preferred return (the "Minimum Return"), then distributions from either net sale or financing proceeds shall be made 80 percent/20 percent to the investors/Principal, respectively;

- If for any reason the investors receive less than their Minimum Return, then Principal shall forfeit his share of distributions until adequate funds are available to pay the investors the Minimum Return;
- Principal shall use good-faith efforts to sell all properties, distribute the net sales proceeds, and wind up the affairs of the Company no later than forty-eight months from the inception date. Principal shall have the right to extend the wind-up date by up to twelve months.
- Regardless of the foregoing, investors shall receive annual cash distributions, if available, at least high enough to pay their tax liabilities from any net income allocated to them from the Company. Such tax distributions, if any, shall count toward the Minimum Return.
- Prior to any property sales or financings, it is anticipated that the investors 6 percent preferred return payments will be funded from their own capital.

Plan of Action/Timetable

The Company looks to raise $1 million from investors during the fall of 2012. Assuming commitments from investors are obtained in time, the Company hopes to begin operations February 2013. The Company will not proceed unless at least $600,000 in commitments is obtained.

The Company is already working on securing contingent purchase agreements for properties that it expects to have in place prior to the date the Company is formed. Such agreements may be assigned to the Company and would allow the Company to accelerate its start-up.

The timetable and steps to set up the Company and begin operations are listed below:

SAMPLE BUSINESS PLAN (NARRATIVE ONLY)

November–December 2012 — Meet with potential investors, obtain preliminary commitments

January–February 2013 — Engage outside legal counsel. Counsel to:
- Form Company as Delaware limited liability company
- Prepare operating agreement
- File for tax registration
- Obtain needed business licenses

Enter into formal Subscription Agreements with investors

Begin property search, possibly enter contingent purchase agreements for properties

Enter into formal agreement for accounting, tax, and administrative services with Quality Back Office Solutions ("QBO"). QBO to:
- Create logo and marketing message; set up website
- Open operating bank account
- Set up accounting systems
- Set up vendor and supplier payment system

March 2013 — Begin property acquisitions and renovations

Market & Competition

The housing market in the United States has been in a downturn since 2008. There have recently been signs of improvement in certain markets, but these signs can best be characterized as "bouncing off the bottom." Furthermore, there are still estimated to be millions more in distressed sales as many houses are still "underwater" and their owners are simply waiting for the banks to take action. As such, there is still a tremendous opportunity to purchase residential properties at large discounts from their 2008 highs.

There are several articles attached as <u>Exhibit C</u> *(not included)* regarding current real estate market conditions that further illustrate that this is an opportune time for the Company to undertake its plans.

There is strong evidence that home values and prices in the target market area are starting to bottom out. Reference is made to the chart on *Trends in Home Values & Prices* attached as <u>Exhibit D</u> *(not included)*. This chart clearly shows that in four of the five target markets that values are stabilizing in 2012. This chart information is graphed by market in <u>Exhibits E.1 to E.5</u> *(not included)*.

Therefore, this is a superb time to implement the Company's strategy. Prices are down in these markets 20 to 30 percent from the peak, so there are still plenty of upsides. Prices are starting to stabilize thus reducing the risk of losses due to further market deterioration.

There are a number of people and businesses conducting similar business activities in the target market area. However, based on firsthand observation, the Principal believes that the number of opportunities to purchase distressed properties exceeds the number of readily available buyers. In addition, once the Company has secured funding, the Principal has already been making arrangements with local realtors who will begin to refer deals directly to the Company.

SAMPLE BUSINESS PLAN (NARRATIVE ONLY)

Capital Needs

The Company is looking to raise $1 million, which will allow the Company to reach an adequate scale to cover overhead and other fixed expenses and to generate a substantial return for its investors. As reflected in the *Cash Flow Projection* in <u>Exhibit A</u> *(not included)*, the primary uses of cash are to fund property purchases and renovation costs.

Business Risks

There are a number of business risks that could negatively impact the Company's ability to achieve its goals and its projected cash flows and distributions to investors. These risks include all of the following, plus others including general economic and business risks.

Housing Prices: Although values and prices appear to have stabilized recently in the Company's target markets and nationally, prices could begin to decrease again. This has already happened once in the spring of 2010, when it appeared that prices were plateauing and starting to increase. However, prices turned negative again, showing the improvements to be temporary and short-lived.

Financing Availability: The Company's success is predicated on selling houses. It is anticipated that the vast majority or possibly even all of the Company's buyers will require mortgage loans. The lack of availability of such loans could have a dramatic negative impact on the Company.

Interest Rates: Increases in interest rates could have a two-fold negative impact. First, it will increase prospective buyer's loan payments, leading to a smaller pool of qualified buyers for the Company's properties. Second, increasing interest rates often have a negative impact on housing prices, which could reduce the Company's selling prices and put pressure on operating margins.

Higher interest rates will also increase loan payments to be made by the Company on any properties that it finances, thus reducing cash flow.

Performance of Managing Member: The Company's management team will be making a significant number of decisions on its own that will ultimately determine whether the Company achieves its goals and projected cash flows.

Material and Subcontractor Costs: Increases in inflation could increase the Company's costs to renovate properties, which would reduce the Company's margins.

Accounting & Administration

The Company has contracted with Quality Back Office (www.goqbo.com) to provide accounting and administration services as follows:
- Monthly financial statement preparation;
- Bill paying;
- Investor reporting;
- Lien waiver processing;
- Investor reporting and communications;
- Year-end tax return and K-1 preparation;
- Maintaining property records and files; and
- Collecting rents.

EXHIBIT B2

SAMPLE BUSINESS PLAN/ FEASIBILTY STUDY

**DOWN ON YOUR LUCK
HOTEL & CASINO
RENO**

**FEASIBILITY STUDY
FOR
TIME-SHARE DEVELOPMENT**

MAY 2001

DOWN ON YOUR LUCK HOTEL & CASINO
FEASIBILITY STUDY FOR TIME-SHARE
INDEX

PROJECT INFORMATION
    PROJECT DESCRIPTION   A
    PRICING SCHEDULE   B
    PROJECT TIMETABLE   NOT INCLUDED
    PRELIMINARY FLOOR PLANS   NOT INCLUDED
    PICTURES OF HOTEL   NOT INCLUDED

MARKET ANALYSIS
    EVALUATION OF MARKET   F
    SUMMARY OF COMPETITION   NOT INCLUDED
    PICTURES OF TIME-SHARES   NOT INCLUDED
    LOCATION OF TIME-SHARES   NOT INCLUDED
    DEMOGRAPHICS   J
    HOTEL OCCUPANCY   NOT INCLUDED
    MARKETING SURVEY   NOT INCLUDED

PROJECT FINANCIAL INFORMATION
    PROJECT PROFORMA   M
    START-UP-COST BUDGET   N

DISCLAIMER: NO REPRESENTATIONS OR WARRANTIES, EXPRESS OR IMPLIED, BY OPERATION OF LAW OR OTHERWISE, ARE MADE REGARDING THE INFORMATION CONTAINED IN THIS FEASIBILITY STUDY. RECEIVING PARTIES SHOULD CONDUCT THEIR OWN INVESTIGATION AND INQUIRIES REGARDING THE INFORMATION CONTAINED HEREIN. ONLY REPRESENTATIONS AND WARRANTIES INCLUDED IN EXECUTED AND DELIVERED DEFINITIVE AGREEMENTS, IF ANY, WILL HAVE LEGAL EFFECT.

SAMPLE BUSINESS PLAN/FEASIBILTY STUDY

DOWN ON YOUR LUCK TIME-SHARE RESORT (the "Resort") PROJECT DESCRIPTION AND EVALUATION

GENERAL

My Company ("My Company") and the Down on Your Luck owner ("Owner") will form a joint venture (the "JV") to develop, market, sell, and manage a time-share resort in the North Tower of the Down on Your Luck Hotel in Reno. Owner will contribute hotel rooms, floor-by-floor, to the JV for conversion into time-share condominium units and subsequent sale to time-share purchasers. Owner will also contribute the ground floor of the North Tower to the JV, which will be converted into a sales and reception center. My Company will manage the JV and, as such, will supervise all sales and marketing activities, oversee financial and administrative matters, supervise resort and POA matters, and obtain financing.

STRATEGY

There are sufficient hotel guest arrivals (approximately 90,000 arrivals during 2000) and casino patrons at the Down on Your Luck Hotel that we will be able to generate a sufficient level of sales tours through in-house marketing programs. This will be the key to the resort's success in that it will allow us to generate a steady stream of sales prospects on-site and will allow us to keep marketing costs low.

We will offer these sales prospects the opportunity to become an owner and enjoy the following:

- A superior one- or two-bedroom unit with significant amenities, including a big-screen television with DVD player; whirlpool tub; a complete, high-quality kitchen with GE

White-on-White appliances; a quality stereo system and quality furnishings and decorating.
- An owner's lounge with billiards, a wet-bar and a home theater, multimedia setup.
- An exercise facility.
- All the privileges of ownership at My Company Resorts, including priority exchange and 50 percent rental discounts at our other resorts.
- Membership in the Exchange Company, which offers time-share owners the ability to exchange their week for a week at other resorts located throughout the world.
- A special cruise program that revolves around exchange of time-share weeks (intervals) for cruises or cruise discounts.
- A "home" casino/hotel with restaurants, a lounge, a convenience store, shows, and a pool.

We believe that we will be offering our customers a resort experience that exceeds their expectations. And just as important, we can make it affordable to them.

The price will be significantly below the competition in Reno at $7,500 for a one-bedroom ("1BR") unit and $9,900 for a two-bedroom ("2BR") unit. We will also offer alternate year usage options, which will bring the 1BR and 2BR prices (for alternates) to $4,900 and $6,400, respectively. These prices will be affordable to households with incomes of $40,000 and higher as we will offer ten-year financing with low monthly payments (see *Pricing and Payment Schedule* included under Tab B).

In summary, we believe that we are offering an outstanding vacation experience that is not otherwise available in this market for a very reasonable price.

SAMPLE BUSINESS PLAN/FEASIBILTY STUDY

RESORT DESCRIPTION AND CONVERSION PLAN

The Down on Your Luck Hotel and Casino is located in Reno. The exact location of the Down on Your Luck is shown on the map titled *Reno* included under Tab I. Pictures of the Down on Your Luck are included under Tab E.

The Down on Your Luck is actually located on two separate blocks and is connected by a sky bridge. The North Tower, which we plan to convert to time-share condominiums, contains twenty-two floors of units and ground-floor storage. The top floor consists of suites, which are used for high rollers. The remaining twenty-one floors contain 378 hotel rooms.

We plan to start with the twenty-first floor and convert the hotel rooms into two 2BR units, four 1BR units, and an owner's lounge. We expect to use one of each type of unit as a model for sales tours. At the same time, we will convert the bulk of the ground floor (approximately seven thousand square feet) into a sales and reception center and offices.

Our preliminary cost estimate for the conversion of the twenty-first floor and the ground floor (sales and reception center) are $454,000 and $650,000, respectively. These estimates include all finishes and FF&E. As such, the total cost for Phase I would be $1.1 million. These figures are rough estimates only; exact numbers will not become available until an architect and designer complete plans, and formal contractor bids are received.

The overall mix of 1BR and 2BR units will ultimately depend on demand considerations. However, we believe that the demand for 1BR units will be high. Therefore, we expect the ultimate build-out to be 172 time-share units with 128-1BR units and 44-2BR units. The conversion factors are as follows:

- 256 hotel rooms into: 128 - 1BR time-share units (2 into 1)
- 132 hotel rooms into: 44 - 2BR time-share units (3 into 1)
- 4 hotel rooms into: An owner's lounge
- 4 hotel rooms into: An exercise facility

The units will be approximately 670 sq. ft. and 1,150 sq. ft. for 1BR and 2 BR units, respectively. A preliminary floor plan for both types of units is included under Tab D.

The sales and reception center will be located on the ground floor and will have an entrance onto Game Street. This area will include a reception/check-in area, sales center, offices, and a staff lounge area. The elevators for the North Tower are accessible from the ground floor, so sales prospects can take the elevator from the sales center to the twenty-first floor to view the 1BR and 2BR models and the owner's lounge area.

MARKETING – TOUR GENERATION

As discussed above, our marketing programs will rely heavily on in-house programs for tour generation. Although the program will evolve over time as we determine what works best, we expect most of the following will be part of the in-house marketing program:

1. We will need a concierge desk in the lobby/casino area, which will be staffed by employees of the JV.

SAMPLE BUSINESS PLAN/FEASIBILTY STUDY

2. Promotional displays will be included in all guest rooms, inviting guests to register for a drawing at the concierge desk. When guests register for the drawing, the concierge will try to convert them to a tour by offering them a gift.
3. The concierge will also make phone calls to hotel guests while on-site, inviting them to stop by the concierge desk to register for the drawing or to receive a gift.
4. We would like a booth in the casino, offering casino patrons the opportunity to receive a gift.
5. We would like the opportunity to take over the activities desk and sell activities ourselves. This would be preferable to letting the current operator remain on-site as we believe that our concierge function needs to be closely coordinated with activity sales. If the current operator remains, we would like to meet with them and propose that they offer their customers (on- and off-site) the opportunity for a discount on the activity that they booked in exchange for taking the time-share tour.
6. Promotional materials will be developed and displayed in the casino, restaurants, and hotel.

As far as the gift that we will offer, we expect to offer fifty to seventy dollars in gaming chips or a discount certificate for the Down on Your Luck restaurants and show. We expect to distribute approximately $600,000 in chips and certificates annually.

SALES

Once we reach stabilized sales, we anticipate a sales line of approximately eighteen to twenty-five people with two to three managers and a director of sales. These people will all be independent contractors working for the JV. The agents will be 100 percent commission, while management will have a portion of their compensation guaranteed.

The sales tour will take an hour and a half to two hours. Prospects will start in the sales center and will be given a complete property tour, including the time-share units, owner's lounge, pool, casino, and restaurants. All tours will end back at the sales center, where the final pitch will be made and all paperwork processed.

Interval pricing is listed above and on the *Pricing and Payment Schedule* included under Tab B.

In terms of selling tactics and incentives, My Company runs a very tight operation. We are a one-price shop, which means that anyone who buys today will get "the" price—the same price that everyone else buys at until My Company approves a price increase.

Our "first-day incentive" is also a fixed program that resort management cannot vary. Generally, we offer "My Company $'s" as the primary "buy today" incentive. We have loaded 5 percent of the sales price ($400 for a 1BR and $500 for a 2BR unit) in the projection for first-day incentives. We also offer the first year's membership in Exchange Company (the exchange company) and in ICE (the cruise exchange company) along with a discount travel certificate from Exchange Company.

MARKET AND COMPETITION

The Reno market and competitive time-share projects are reviewed in a separate narrative titled *Evaluation of Market and Competition* included under Tab F.

SAMPLE BUSINESS PLAN/FEASIBILTY STUDY

ORGANIZATION & PERSONNEL

All on-site personnel will be either employees or independent contractors of the JV. Typically, My Company has three senior management personnel at each of its resorts:

> Director of Sales – responsible for all sales and marketing operations for the resort and reporting directly to Marta Schwartz, Copresident, My Company Resorts

> Resort Controller – responsible for all budgeting, accounting, cash management, and administrative areas for the resort and reporting directly to Freida Payne, My Company CFO.

> Resort Operations Manager – responsible for the hospitality side of the resort and reporting directly to Marley Harley, Hospitality Manager, My Company

In addition to the sales staffing discussed above, we anticipate the following additional personnel on-site once we reach stabilized sales levels:
- Four to six sales support staff – quality assurance, loan and escrow, and reception.
- One to two marketing personnel.
- Staff for our concierge desk and one OPC booth in the casino.
- Two to four finance/accounting personnel.
- A hospitality manager and, assuming we have a separate check-in, applicable front desk personnel.

All of the above personnel would be hourly or salaried, except the concierge and OPC booth personnel, who will be partly or completely commission. My Company management will be in daily contact with the resort management team. My Company will make all important decisions.

FINANCING

There are two kinds of financing that will be needed by the JV to successfully develop and sell time-share intervals at the Down on Your Luck.

First, we will need a renovation loan, which will be used to pay for the cost of unit renovations and the sales and reception center remodeling. As we are starting with only one floor and the sales and reception center, we should only need a $1.1 million revolving loan. This loan will be repaid from the sales of intervals on a release-price basis. The exact release price remains to be negotiated with the banks. The issue on the release prices will be the period of time that the sales center and owner's lounge costs can be amortized over. As the total costs involved are not huge, the ultimate impact of our negotiations will not be huge, but there is some potential that some additional cash negatives could be generated during the start-up period from a more aggressive loan pay-down schedule.

The rate on this loan will probably be prime + 2 percent. We used prime + 2.5 percent in the projection to be conservative. Interest will be payable monthly. The lenders typically require one point upfront as a loan fee.

The second loan will be a receivables or hypothecation loan. This loan will need to provide for $8 to $10 million in advances over the first eighteen months of sales. The lender will make advances monthly in amounts equal to 90 percent of "qualified" time-share receivables, which we receive from our purchasers. The lenders take the note payments that our owners make on their notes in full satisfaction of our monthly payment requirements on the hypothecation loan. The interest rate on this loan will probably be prime + 1.25 percent, but we used + 1.624 percent in the Proforma. Loan fees will likely be .5 percent upfront and .5 percent with each advance.

As discussed in the *Evaluation of Market and Competition* under Tab F, the time-share financing environment is not good at this time. However, My Company has just completed a $28 million loan facility for one of its resorts, and our lender relationships are strong. Additionally, our primary lender displayed a high level of interest in a recent visit to the Down on Your Luck.

PROJECTIONS

The most critical period of any new time-share resort is the start-up period. During this time period, which can range from six to nine months, the:

- Sales staff is getting comfortable with the sales presentation and with selling the product.
- Developer is handling construction issues, fine-tuning the product offering and pricing, and fire fighting on a number of fronts

- Marketing personnel are getting accustomed to properly setting up tours.
- MIS, financial, and accounting systems are being set up and tested under fire.

As such, it is important that adequate working capital be set aside to ensure that the project can survive this start-up period. A budget for the start-up period titled *Down on Your Luck Time-share Start-up Costs* is included under Tab Q. The total of these start-up costs needs to be contributed as equity upon formation of the JV.

The *Down on Your Luck Time-share Proforma* is attached under Tab P. This Proforma reflects cash flow and net income for the Resort for a ten-year sellout period and ten-year note amortization period for all financed sales.

The net cash flow over the twenty-year projection period is approximately $60 million. This figure is after payment of My Company' base management fee of 3 percent of sales but before payments of My Company "net fee," which is equal to 8 percent of net cash flow and is before payment to Owner of their contribution credit and preferred return.

The IRR's on each party's cash investment are 50 percent and 103 percent for My Company and Owner, respectively. However, this IRR does not reflect the value of Owner's hotel room contributions. Assuming the hotel rooms are valued at $12,500 each ($5 million in total for the North Tower) and using the timetable in the Proforma to calculate the net present value of the hotel room contribution, the IRR to Owner is 35 percent.

SAMPLE BUSINESS PLAN/FEASIBILTY STUDY

SUMMARY

We have a unique product at an affordable price with a plethora of potential customers right on property. It would seem difficult for vacation ownership at the Down on Your Luck to fail. The primary risks that are discussed in the *Evaluation of the Market and Competition* relate to the propensity to buy, when rental options are cheaper or even free. Although this is certainly a fair concern, we believe that the vacation ownership product that we have planned for the Down on Your Luck will be a compelling purchase for enough people that we can have a very successful project.

DOWN ON YOUR LUCK VACATION OWNERSHIP EVALUATION OF MARKET & COMPETITION

General

Generally, time-share development in RN has been limited. RN has three million visitors annually but only has around a dozen time-share resorts. Compare this to Orlando where thirty-seven million visitors annually support approximately fifty-five different time-share resorts. The possible undersupply of time-share resorts in RN was pointed out in both a 1997 study, *The Nevada Time-share Industry: An Industry Overview and Economic Impact Analysis*, which was published by ARDA (the time-share developer's association), and in a 1998 study, *Resort Timesharing and Gaming: A survey of Resort Time-share Owners in Atlantic City, Las Vegas, and Reno* by RCI Consulting. These studies focused the industry on RN and the significant time-share opportunities in the market.

A summary of each study is included herein, one under Tab V and the other under Tab W.

These studies also point out the benefits to the gaming industry from time-share. Specifically, that time-share owners:

- stay longer than rental guests;
- spend two times more on nongaming activities;
- have a 40 percent greater gaming budget; and
- are more likely to gamble.

Since these studies were published, there have been approximately six new time-share resorts that have begun sales in RN and dozens

SAMPLE BUSINESS PLAN/FEASIBILTY STUDY

more that have been discussed and evaluated. Generally, almost every second-tier RN hotel/casino has looked at conversion. Many time-share companies have also been actively looking at sites and possible condo, apartment, or motel/hotel conversions. Although there has been a lot of study and discussion, the actual number of projects is still somewhat limited. This is due to a number of factors, including the high cost of land, where most of the time-share companies have focused their efforts. Additionally, the conversion of the second-tier hotel/casinos requires much more capital and interest carry than most of the time-share companies can handle financially. (Generally, the development of time-share resorts is phased, keeping inventory—real estate—costs manageable.)

Other Reno Time-share Resorts

A summary of the existing time-share companies and resorts in RN is included under Tab G. This summary, titled *Summary of Time-share Competition*, also lists potential new resort developments. There are no existing projects downtown. The closest seem to be several miles away in the new suburban areas. The existing resorts include both high-rise towers and two- or three-story apartment-type complexes.

Although there are no resorts located downtown today, our outside legal counsel in RN has told us that another company has inquired of a local real estate/land-use consultant about conversion of a downtown hotel. If someone else is following along the same path, it's probably both good and bad: good because it helps validate our plan that someone else sees the same market opportunity; bad because it may foreclose some downtown market relationships. Overall, since we are relying primarily on in-house marketing programs (described below), we do not believe that another downtown project should impact our decision on whether to proceed with the Down on Your Luck.

Characteristics of Reno Time-share Resorts and Customers

Time-share sales for 2000 in RN were likely in the range of $70 million to $90 million, which is less than 2 percent of total US sales. The average interval price in RN was approximately $11,700 in 1997, which is higher than the national average. The average is a function of studios at $7,200; 1BRs at $9,300 and 2BRs at $12,300. Premiums on alternate-year inventory sales help drive up the average price. Pricing has certainly escalated from 1997 to today. Maintenance fees average $407 and $313 for a 2BR and 1BR, respectively.

As far as the Down on Your Luck, we are projecting sales conservatively at approximately $10 million at stabilization. This is certainly a small share of the RN market and will probably increase the size of the market. From a national perspective, sales at the Down on Your Luck are extremely minor.

Down on Your Luck pricing is planned to be well below the existing market at $7,500 for a 1BR and $9,900 for a 2BR. However, it is important to note that the target customer for the Down on Your Luck is the Downtown RN customer, which likely has a lower income level.

Down on Your Luck maintenance fees will also be well below the market. We expect the 1BR fee to be between $175 and $250, while the 2BR will be in the $250 to $300 range.

SAMPLE BUSINESS PLAN/FEASIBILTY STUDY

Our planned amenities for the Down on Your Luck Vacation Ownership Resort compare very favorably with this list of amenities. Specifically, the Down on Your Luck already has a pool, convenience store, restaurants, and a casino. We are planning hot tubs for the units, an owner's lounge, and a health club/exercise room. The only items omitted are the tennis court(s) and the kids' center/play area, which we do not believe are necessary.

We do believe that the project would benefit from an improvement of the pool area. A simple expansion of the deck area and adding a hot tub and some additional lounge chairs and umbrella tables would have a significant positive impact. Also the walkway from the tower to the pool could use some improvement.

Time-share Marketing Programs

Many of the existing time-share companies rely heavily on OPC (off-premise contact) booths in casinos and retail outlets for purposes of generating sales prospects. The relationships between several of the time-share companies and the hotel/casinos are identified in the *Summary of Time-share Competition*. These efforts are entirely concentrated on suburban hotel/casinos and retail outlets. Given the penetration of these marketing locations and relationships, it is doubtful that we would be able to penetrate in this area, assuming we wanted to.

Several companies also have telemarketing operations that offer discounted vacations in exchange for taking a time-share tour while in RN. Generally, these tours are higher quality (i.e., a greater percentage actually purchase an interval) than the OPC tours.

New Business Landmines

As in other markets, there are a number of independent marketing (tour-generation) companies that effectively sell tours to various developers. Generally, as a newcomer to a market, only the lowest quality tours would be available to buy. However, we have had success in several markets buying tours, and this option should be evaluated carefully once we begin sales as a supplement to our in-house tour-generation program.

As discussed in the *Project Description and Evaluation*, the Down on Your Luck will be able to generate adequate tour flow from hotel guests and casino patrons—an "in-house marketing program." This program is critical to the success of the project as outside tour generation would be expensive and difficult. We are currently operating an in-house program at one of our resorts. Through this program we have been able to convert approximately 35 percent of our rental guests to tours and to close (sell an interval) approximately 13 to 15 percent of these tours. This program allows us to operate at 35 percent sales and marketing costs as a percentage of sales at the resort, which compares very favorably with the industry average of 50 percent.

Risks

The primary risks are: (1) lower hotel guest arrivals and (2) prospects unwilling to buy in a market where hotel rooms are inexpensive or free.

An economic downturn or the impact of Indian casinos in CA could have a negative impact on Down on Your Luck occupancies and, hence, on our projected tour flow and sales pace. Partially mitigating this risk is Owner's commitment to operating its properties at 90 percent plus occupancy. Additionally, the occupancy

SAMPLE BUSINESS PLAN/FEASIBILTY STUDY

for the past three years has been at a level that would provide sufficient tour prospects for our sales operation.

The second point related to a lack of motivation to purchase is probably the reason that many time-share developers have avoided RN in the past. It is a legitimate concern.

In evaluating this risk the following countervailing points should be considered:

First, the opening of the new suburban resorts reflects that fact that people are willing to pay a higher price for a quality product in the greater RN market. Years ago many people erroneously thought that it would not be possible to charge $100 for a hotel room in RN.

Second, the sales success of several new high-rise condominiums reflects that there is a market for second homes in RN. Generally, where people are willing to pay for second homes (or condos), there is the potential for time-share.

One could reasonably argue that both of these examples are at the higher end of the market and that the lower end would be most price-sensitive, thus making them more reluctant to part with their money for a time-share when inexpensive rooms are available. Possibly true, but consider these points.

The significant success of time-share resorts converting lower-end market customers to time-share purchasers in markets like Daytona Beach, FL, Myrtle Beach, SC, and Branson, MO, where hotel/motel rooms are available at very low prices.

If the product is affordable to the lower-income prospect and offers a real value over the less expensive alternative, we believe the customer will buy. We believe that the Down on Your Luck Vacation Ownership Resort will offer this kind of compelling value.

Overall Evaluation of Competition and Market

Although there are a significant number of potential future RN time-share resorts, the competition is somewhat limited at this today. Additionally, today there is no competition for either marketing relationships or product in the downtown market. There is also a strong employment base, which should make staffing the sales and marketing areas less of a challenge than in certain other resort markets. The key to the success of the project is the in-house marketing program to hotel and casino guests. This program will bring us a better quality sales tour and will keep our marketing costs at a low level. There are very few time-share projects in RN that have the luxury of operating an in-house tour-generation program. This will give the Down on Your Luck Vacation Ownership project a significant competitive advantage.

SAMPLE BUSINESS PLAN/FEASIBILTY STUDY

DOWN ON YOUR LUCK TIME-SHARE HOTEL GUEST DEMOGRAPHICS

Employment Status	
Employed	48.70%
Retired	40.00%
Homemaker	4.00%
Unemployed	6.70%
Student	0.70%
Total	100.10%

Education	
Grade School	3.30%
High School	50.70%
Technical Trade Schc	2.00%
Some College	24.70%
College Graduate	18.00%
Graduate School	1.30%
	100.00%

Household Incomes	
< 20.0	10.90%
20.0 - 29.9	15.80%
30.0 - 39.9	28.80%
40.0 - 49.9	22.30%
50.0 - 59.9	10.00%
60.0 - 69.9	5.80%
70.0 - 79.9	2.70%
80.0 - 89.9	1.40%
90.0 - 100.0+	2.30%
	100.00%

Age	
21-29	6.70%
30-39	11.40%
40-49	16.80%
50-59	26.20%
60-64	16.10%
65 & Older	22.80%
	100.00%

Ethnic Group	
Asian	2.00%
Black	8.60%
Hispanic	4.70%
Native American	2.00%
White	82.70%
	100.00%

Have Children Under 21	
Yes	15.50%
No	84.50%
	100.00%

Marital Status	
Married	58.00%
Single	17.30%
Separated or Divorcec	11.40%
Widowed	13.30%
	100.00%

DOWN ON YOUR LUCK TIME-SHARE NET CASH FLOW PROJECTION

Down on Your Luck Hotel
Timeshare Proforma
Statement of Cash Flow

	2002	2003	2004	2005	2006
Sources of Cash					
Mortgage collections	323,010	1,328,434	2,717,110	4,157,259	5,657,038
Hypothecation advances	2,793,640	5,902,023	6,108,293	6,347,211	6,624,037
Excess hypo fundings	-	-	2,100,000	-	4,000,000
Cash sales	189,966	406,893	432,359	459,772	489,430
Down payments	360,935	773,096	821,483	873,567	929,917
Renovation loan advances	1,100,000	1,133,000	1,750,485	1,202,000	1,857,090
Total sources	4,767,551	9,543,446	13,929,730	13,039,809	19,557,512
Uses of Cash					
Hypothecation loan repayment	323,010	1,328,434	2,717,110	4,157,259	5,657,038
Renovation costs	1,100,000	1,133,000	1,750,485	1,202,000	1,857,090
Renovation loan releases	810,000	1,403,000	1,403,000	1,403,000	1,403,000
Renovation interest expense	16,675	17,825	22,280	30,703	45,256
First day incentives	189,966	406,893	432,359	459,772	489,430
Marketing and sales expense	2,255,846	4,020,099	4,271,710	4,542,550	4,835,566
Administration expense	360,935	773,096	821,483	873,567	929,917
POA subsidy/Resort operation	25,000	50,000	35,000	30,000	25,000
Lender fees	13,968	29,510	30,541	31,736	33,120
Total uses	5,095,400	9,161,857	11,483,968	12,730,587	15,275,417
Annual Cash surplus (deficiency)	(327,849)	381,589	2,445,762	309,222	4,282,095

Only five years shown due to space limitations.

SAMPLE BUSINESS PLAN/FEASIBILTY STUDY

DOWN ON YOUR LUCK TIME-SHARE
START-UP-COST BUDGET

	Budget
Marketing & Sales	
State sales registration(s)	30,000
Promotional materials	35,000
Sales materials	50,000
Pre-sale office/space costs	10,000
Recruiting/hiring/training costs	50,000
Pre-sale salaries/wages	50,000
General & Administrative	
Pre-sale office/space costs	5,000
Recruiting/hiring/training costs	35,000
Pre-sale salaries/wages	25,000
Systems & installation	35,000
Other	
Financing costs:	
Loan fees	85,000
Legal	40,000
Organization costs:	
Partnership/LLC documents	25,000
Condo documents	40,000
Legal organization	10,000
Building & design costs	50,000
Miscellaneous	75,000
Start-up Costs	650,000
Operating losses prior to stabilization	350,000
Total start-up	1,000,000
Working capital/minimum cash balance	250,000
Total Cash Requirement	**1,250,000**

EXHIBIT C

SAMPLE MONTHLY CASH FLOW BUDGET

CASH RECEIPTS BUDGET - PAGE 1 OF 5

	ASSUMPTIONS		Totals	Mth 1	Mth 2	Mth 3
Tours						
Total	Net Closing Rate	Source Stabilized	11,700	1,000	1,250	1,250
In-house concierge	20.00%	25.00%	2,716			391
Purchased OPC	18.00%	25.00%	3,738	455	568	391
Purch OPC - "Retread"	16.00%	10.00%	1,495	182	227	156
Purchased Mini-vac	22.00%	20.00%	2,991	364	455	313
In-house Mini-vacs	24.00%	20.00%	760			
Total Tours		100%	11,700	1,000	1,250	1,250
Deals Written			2,296	191	239	242
Deals Closed			2,245	143	227	241
Notes - Financed Deals	30.00%		673	43	68	72
Cumulative Notes				43	111	183
# of cumulative defaults					1	3
Notes after defaults					110	180
Ave Deal Price	$4,395	Net price				
TTG dues & doc	$600					
Sales (closed)			9,866,261	629,284	996,366	1,060,512
Gross sales (w/dues + docs)			11,213,190	715,193	1,132,389	1,205,292
			0			
Cash Receipts						
Cash Deals - price	70.00%		6,906,382	440,499	697,457	742,359
Dues & docs		no financing	1,346,930	85,909	136,023	144,780
Down Payments - price	10.00%		295,988	18,879	29,891	31,815
Note reserve releases						
Hypo Advances	64.00%		1,704,890	108,740	172,172	183,257
Loan defaults	3.00%	/mth	(63,508)	0	0	(7,472)
Total Cash Receipts			10,190,682	654,027	1,035,542	1,094,739
			0			

Only three months shown due to space limitations.

SAMPLE MONTHLY CASH FLOW BUDGET

COST OF PRODUCT & SALES COSTS BUDGET - PAGE 2 OF 5

Cost of Sales						
Product cost and dues	$600		1,346,930	85,909	136,023	144,780
less: rebate	260		(583,670)	(37,227)	(58,943)	(62,738)
Total Cost of Sales	7.50%		763,260	48,682	77,080	82,042
			0			
Sales Dept						
Project Director						
Base salary	12,500	/mth	150,000	12,500	12,500	12,500
Override	1.75%		172,660	11,012	17,436	18,559
Director of sales						
Base	4,000	/Mth miniumum	0			
Override	1.50%		147,994	9,439	14,945	15,908
Sales Reps	12.00%		1,183,951	75,514	119,564	127,261
Podium	4.00%		394,650	25,171	39,855	42,420
Spiff account	2.00%		197,325	12,586	19,927	21,210
Bonuses	1.00%		98,663	6,293	9,964	10,605
Taxes & Benefits	8.00%		187,619	12,201	18,735	19,877
Commission credit (defaults)			(9,493)	0	(527)	(1,055)
Consultants/sales trainers	1.00%		98,663	6,293	9,964	10,605
Total Selling Costs	25.70%		2,622,032	171,010	262,363	277,891
			0			

Only three months shown due to space limitations.

MARKETING COST BUDGET - PAGE 3 OF 5

Marketing Department						
Personnel						
Marketing Mgr	1.50%	override	147,994	9,439	14,945	15,908
Control Room (2 people)	100	Hrs/week				
Wages	$12		61,714	5,143	5,143	5,143
Premiums Person	45	Hrs/week				
Wages	$12		27,771	2,314	2,314	2,314
Van Drivers	80	Hrs/week				
Wages	$15		61,714	5,143	5,143	5,143
Taxes & Benefits	8%		23,936	1,763	2,204	2,281
Promotion						
Misc gifts/trinkets	$30,000	/yr	30,000	2,500	2,500	2,500
Advertising	$12,000	/yr	12,000	1,000	1,000	1,000
Direct Mailers		/yr	0	0	0	0
Invites and other	$12,000	/yr	12,000	1,000	1,000	1,000
Internet Site	$12,000	/yr	12,000	1,000	1,000	1,000
OPC/Phone Room Set Up			165,000	15,000	15,000	15,000
First Day Incentives	5.00%		493,313	31,464	49,818	53,026
In house tour Cost	$275	/in-house tour	746,797	0	0	107,422
Purchased OPC Cost	$360	/purch tour	1,345,807	163,636	204,545	140,625
Purch OPC "Retread"	$230	/purch tour	343,928	41,818	52,273	35,938
Purch Mini-vac Cost	$400	/purch MV tour	1,196,273	145,455	181,818	125,000
In House Mini-vac Cost	$350	/in house MV	266,000	0	0	0
Total Marketing Costs	48.54%		4,946,247	426,676	538,704	513,298
			0			

Only three months shown due to space limitations.

SAMPLE MONTHLY CASH FLOW BUDGET

ADMIN COST BUDGET - PAGE 4 OF 5

Administration Department						
Rent	240,000	/yr	240,000	20,000	20,000	20,000
Utilities	24,000	/yr	24,000	2,000	2,000	2,000
Telephone and HS Internet	12,000	/yr	12,000	1,000	1,000	1,000
Software licensing fees	12,000	/yr	12,000	1,000	1,000	1,000
Insurance	12,000	/yr	12,000	1,000	1,000	1,000
Escrow/Title work	$35	/sale	78,571	5,011	7,935	8,445
Office Supplies	24,000	/yr	24,000	2,000	2,000	2,000
Credit Card Discounts	3.00%	of cash receipts	256,479	16,359	25,901	27,569
Credit card reserves	10.00%	max $100k	100,928	62,928	38,000	
Credit check costs	1.00%	of cash receipts	101,907	6,540	10,355	10,947
Coffee/Food service	$6	/tour	70,200	6,000	7,500	7,500
Cleaning	18,000	/yr	18,000	1,500	1,500	1,500
FedX Postage etc	18,000	/yr	18,000	1,500	1,500	1,500
Note Servicing Costs						
Setup	$5	/note	3,367	215	340	362
Monthly	$5	/note/mth	21,520	215	550	900
Misc	12,000	/yr	12,000	1,000	1,000	1,000
Annual Audit	20,000	/yr	20,000			
Memberships/Community Rel	18,000	/yr	18,000	1,500	1,500	1,500
Hiring and recruiting costs	18,000	/yr	18,000	1,500	1,500	1,500
MIS Support/equipment	18,000	/yr	18,000	1,500	1,500	1,500
Professional Fees	12,000	/yr	12,000	1,000	1,000	1,000

Only three months shown due to space limitations.

ADMIN PERSONNEL COST BUDGET & BUDGET TOTALS - PAGE 5 OF 5

Personnel Costs							
Admin/VLO/Contracts							
Admin Director	60,000	/yr		60,000	5,000	5,000	5,000
	0.50%	override		49,331	3,146	4,982	5,303
QA #1	40,000	/yr		40,000	3,333	3,333	3,333
	0.25%	override		24,666	1,573	2,491	2,651
QA #2	24,000	/yr		24,000	2,000	2,000	2,000
	0.13%	override		12,333	787	1,245	1,326
QA #3	24,000	/yr		24,000	2,000	2,000	2,000
	0.13%	override		12,333	787	1,245	1,326
Contracts	40,000	/yr		40,000	3,333	3,333	3,333
	0.13%	override		12,333	787	1,245	1,326
Support							
Receptionist	60	Hrs/week					
Wages	$10			30,857	2,571	2,571	2,571
Taxes and Benefits	8.00%			26,388	2,025	2,356	2,414
Employee Relations	12,000	/yr		12,000	1,000	1,000	1,000
Admin/Accounting/Payroll/Tax							
QBO Base Fee	1,000	/mth		12,000	1,000	1,000	1,000
QBO Per Deal Fee	30	/deal		67,346	4,295	6,801	7,239
Total G&A Costs		15.10%		1,538,560	167,407	167,685	134,045
				0			
Net Cash Flow - Front Line		3.15%		320,583	(159,747)	(10,289)	87,462
Net Cash Flow - Exits (NOT INCLUDED)				528,234	45,446	56,807	56,608
Net Cash Flow - Total		8.33%		848,817	(114,302)	46,518	144,070
				0			

Only three months shown due to space limitations.

EXHIBIT D

TWELVE-WEEK CASH FLOW FORECAST

ROLLING 12-WEEK CASH FLOW
(4 WEEKS SHOWN)

	6/27/2008	7/4/2008	7/11/2008	7/18/2008
TS Sales	62,000	50,000	40,000	30,000
Rooms	15,000	15,000	17,500	12,000
Spa	2,500	2,500	3,000	1,750
F&B	20,000	17,500	18,000	12,000
Total Cash Receipts	99,500	85,000	78,500	55,750
Payroll Expense				
Sales Commissions	12,000	10,000	8,000	7,500
F&B	17,000		17,000	
Spa	14,800		14,800	
Sales admin	3,000		3,000	
Tour cost	20,417	16,042	11,667	21,000
Capital improvements		2,790		
Front dsk/HSK allocation		30,000		
Accts Payable				
Hotel	3,500	3,500	3,500	3,500
Spa	4,500	4,500	4,500	4,500
F&B	14,200	14,200	14,200	14,200
Timeshare	14,000	14,000	14,000	14,000
Total Cash Disbursments	103,417	95,032	90,667	64,700
Net Cash Flow	(3,917)	(10,032)	(12,167)	(8,950)
Beginning Cash	45,876	41,959	31,928	19,761
Ending Cash	41,959	31,928	19,761	10,811

EXHIBIT E

LIST OF LANDMINES

1. *Many businesses fail not because of bad ideas, but because of poor execution.* (p.v)
2. *If the idea for the business can't be stated in two to three sentences so the "average" person can understand it, it probably isn't going to work. Said another way, if the customer can't easily understand the business, it will likely fail.* (p.1)
3. *Minimize your investment of time and money until you can determine that the things that you cannot control can get done.* (p.6)
4. *If you don't have a plan, you don't really know where you are going.* (p.8)
5. *Even in today's world, investors still bet on people. As <u>owner/managers</u>, you must be able to demonstrate clearly that your team is well suited to make the business successful.* (p.13)
6. *Approach the real estate needs of your business in a methodical and professional manner or lose a chunk of the business's <u>investment capital</u> before the business even opens. Don't try to do things on the cheap.* (p.16)
7. *The start-up-cost budget needs to include a contingency line to cover unforeseen items, or your cost estimates will be too low.* (p.18)

LIST OF LANDMINES

8. *Use cash flow for budgeting, not income and expenses. Make sure you watch the first couple months and get the timing of receipts and payments correct. Generally, cash will go out much quicker than you think and come in much slower. (p.24)*
9. *The person asking for money wears the tie; the person with the money gets to wear whatever he or she wants. (p.28)*
10. *For any type of company besides a corporation, the owners of the company pay the income taxes, whether they take any cash out of the company or not. (p.37)*
11. *Watch for upcoming changes in the tax code. Generally, personal and corporate rates are pretty similar now. However, there is significant pressure to reduce corporate rates in connection with cutting loopholes and increasing personal rates. This may create a situation where it is advantageous to use a corporate entity for tax purposes. (p.41)*
12. *Don't lose sight of this one fact: the most important thing in business is cash. (p.45)*
13. *The decision to <u>optimize</u> is critically important. If you decide to optimize, interview multiple firms and make sure that your financial commitments are tied to results before entering into any agreements. (p.53)*
14. *Make sure you are advertising to people who may be interested in your product. (p.61)*
15. *Make sure that you put in proper metrics for measuring your marketing expense versus your results. (p.66)*
16. *A marketing program should evolve with the company. (p.67)*
17. *There is no guarantee that you can sell your product or service for more than it costs! (p.71)*
18. *Pricing is more art than science. If possible, start at the lower end of the range. Monitor the impact of price changes closely. (p.74)*
19. *Salespeople are driven by cash, really not much else. Keep their commission structure simple, calculate commissions on gross sales, and pay early and on time to recruit and retain the best. (p.78)*

New Business Landmines

20. *Don't let your financial people build an overly detailed accounting system. Build a system that allows the business to file its taxes and, more importantly, to provide owners/managers the information that they need to make decisions and manage cash. (p.81)*
21. *It is impossible to comply with all government regulations, but it is stupid not to comply with any. (p.85)*
22. *Don't fall into a trap. Declare your income (even cash sales!) for taxes, and then be aggressive on tax deductions. (p.89)*
23. *If you do everything your attorney tells you, you will probably fail. (p.91)*
24. *Lawsuits make attorneys rich, not the litigants. (p.92)*
25. *Fighting lawsuits endlessly is a waste of time and money. Find the right time—usually after you throw a few punches—and then settle them. (p.94)*
26. *Ignore sexual harassment at your own risk. (p.97)*
27. *Simply assume the seller of a business is lying, and you will have no surprises afterward. (p.103)*
28. *Your attorney may not understand this, but businesses can't distribute profits; they can only distribute cash. (p.115)*
29. *Assume nothing; instead insist that all owner/managers state in writing their roles and responsibilities, including how much cash they will invest in the business. (p.120)*
30. *Before getting married to a business partner, a family member or otherwise, you must negotiate and provide for the divorce in writing. (p.121)*
31. *You may not be the best person to run your own business! (p.129)*
32. *Stop answering your phone every time it rings, and that applies to texts and e-mails too! (p.130)*

www.ingramcontent.com/pod-product-compliance
Lightning Source LLC
Chambersburg PA
CBHW051648170526
45167CB00001B/382